The Illustrated Encyclopædia of
ARABIA

The Illustrated Encyclopædia of Arabia
published by
Stacey International
128 Kensington Church Street, London W8 4BH
Tel: +44 (0)207 221 7166 Fax: +44 (0)207 792 9288
Website: www.stacey-international.co.uk
E-mail: info@stacey-international.co.uk
© 2008 Mary Beardwood
First published in 2001 as
The Children's Encyclopædia of Arabia
Reprinted 2002
Revised & reprinted 2008

ISBN: 978-1-905299-94-2

A catalogue record for this book is available from the
British Library.

Printed in China *by* C&C Offset Printing Co., Ltd.
Designed by Kitty Carruthers

THE ILLUSTRATED ENCYCLOPÆDIA OF ARABIA

Mary Beardwood

STACEY
INTERNATIONAL

ACKNOWLEDGEMENTS

Compiling *The Illustrated Encyclopaedia of Arabia* has been a team effort with contributions from a variety of sources. I have been assisted by many people who are specialists in their own field. All of them were willing to share their knowledge of Arabia, advise on the text and check it for accuracy. I am deeply grateful to them, for the book could not have been written without their patience and attention to detail. In particular I would like to thank the following:

Seashells, Horst Kauch, Dr Sandy Fowler; **endangered mammals**, Dr Andrew Spalton, David Insall, Roddy Jones, Moaz Shawab; **mammals**, Dr David Harrison, Mike Smith, The Arabian Wildlife Centre, Sharjah (EPAA); **reptiles**, Dr Marycke Jongbloed; **camels and camel racing**, Dr Lulu Skidmore, Dr Billah, Dr Ullrich Wenery; **Arabian horses**, Rod Hamey; **falconry**, Dr David Remple, Theri Bailey, E.R.W.D.A; **butterflies and moths**, Dr Mike Gillett; **fossils**, Valerie Chalmers, Gary Feulner; **construction and superstructures**, Simon Crisp, Kevin Hall, Chris Lambert, Al Nakheel; **customs and traditions**, Nada Eid al-Kindi, Kamal Sultan, Shawqi Sultan, Ino Ewert; **traditional weaving**, Gigi Crocker-Jones; **archaeology**, Christian Velde, Walid Yassin, Dr Derek Kennet, Michelle Ziolkowski; **masters of the sea**, Dr D McNaughton (the stars), Captain Bill Nelson, Captain Arthur Jarman, Barry Harmsworth (dhow racing); **Islamic architecture**, Dr. Paolo Costa; **bees and bee keeping**, Joss Schoenmakers, The Arabian Wildlife Centre, Sharjah (EPPA); **insects**, Gary Feulner, Kevin Thompson, The Arabian Wildlife Centre, Sharjah (EPPA); **Islam**, Laila Dhia; **plants/date palms**, Dr Reza Khan, Dr Marycke Jongbloed, David Insall, Dr Helal al Kabi, Khalid Alhudaib; **fish, fishing**, Simon Martin, Mark Beech; **water**, David Insall; **whales, dolphins, turtles**, Robert Baldwin; **dugongs**, Dr Anthony Preen; **birds**, Colin Richardson, Kevin Hyland; **the oil industry**, Dr Jamal Barghouti.

In addition to these specialists, many friends also participated in the effort. They lent books, donated photographs and gathered information. For some of them Arabia is their homeland and they have lived through the recent history themselves. Others have spent many years working there and have much knowledge and experience of the area. All of them share a love and respect for their own corner of it. Space prevents me from mentioning them all individually but every contribution has helped make the book a real community project.
Mary Beardwood

The following artists are gratefully acknowledged for their contributions:

Main illustrator, Sue Granter; **mosques**, Margaret Chandler; **bird illustrations**, Frank Jarvis; **insect illustrations**, reproduced from *Insects of Eastern Arabia*, Allan Walker; **mammals**, Dr David Harrison and Sally Wilson for permission to reproduce colour plates and drawings from *Mammals of the Gulf*; Ministry of Information, Oman for permission to reproduce drawings from *Oman, a Seafaring Nation*.

The following photographers are gratefully acknowledged for their contributions:

Charles & Pat Aithie, 15(tr), 17(b), 32/3(t)(m), 33(tr&br), 74(tl); Khalid Alhudaib, 56(bl), (bm); Aramco, 149(br); Simon Aspinall, 11(tl), 87(tm), 115(tl), 116(m3), 123(ml); Mrs N al Kindi, 76(bl); Dr Tom Bailey, 70(m); Robert Baldwin: for permission to reprint photographs from *Whales and Dolphins of Oman*; Mary Beardwood, 10(mr), 13(tr), (bl), 15(tl), (mr,br), 18(tr), 29(ml), 30(mr), 48(tr), 50(br), 54(br), 65(tr), 64(bl,br), 72(t), 73(b,ml), 70(ml), 80(tr), 81(tl), 87(bl), 100(t), 118(b3), 119b3), 121(ml,mr,bm,bl, br), 127(tr); Gunnar Bemert, 60, 61, 94/5(bm), 155(b), 132(m,bl); Bibliothèque Nationale, Paris 44 (tr); Kevin Budd (Arabian Wildlife Centre, Sharjah) 91(br), 101(tl), 105(tl), 129(m); Sue Kitty Carruthers 8, 62-3; Chapman, 34(t), 120(bl); Wendy Cocker, 155(t); Beryl Comar, 127(m); Kevin Cook, 156(ml); Ian Curtis, 122(br), 141(tl); Neil Curtis, 129(bl); Alan Dickson, 103(ml), 140(m), 141(tm), 145(bl), 147(tm), 148(tr), 149(bl), 151(tl,ml); Dubai International Marine Club, 49(bl), 161(ml); Mohamed Durrani, (negatives in the archives of Sharjah heritage department) 58/9(b), 81(b); Iris Edkins, 32(bl), 59(mr); Jane Edmonds (Arabian Wildlife Centre, Sharjah) 95(mr), 98(t, 99(br); Henne & Jens Eriksen, 4(t), 108(tl,tr), 109(bl), 110(l), 112(t,mr,ml), 113(br), 114(l), 115(bl), 123(tl,tr,bl); ERWDA, 70(tr), 71(mr), 128(br); Ino Ewart, 61(tl), 76-7, 79(b), 80(bl); Simon Ferrey, 85(mr); Gary Feulner, 11(mr), 105(tr), 122(b3), 142(bl) 148(ml,mr), 149(mr); Sandy Fowler, 127(mr); Dr Andrew Gardner, 105(bl); David Gillespie, 36(tr); Godolphin Stables, 75(mr); Dr Albert Le Grain, 145(ml); Rod Hamey, 75(bl); Carole Harris, 127(t), 134, 135, 136, 137(ml,mr); Ruth Hawley, 47(bm,br), 66, 67(bl); Ann Holt, 128(ml); Marycke Jongbloed, 87(tl), 91(bl), 104, 119, 145(m), 149(ml); Jumeirah Beach Hotel (Patrouille de France),W J Atkins, 162(ml); Lamjid El Kefi, 16(ml), 26(tr), 28(tr), 33(br), 40-1(t), 42(tl,tr), 43(bm), 51(tr,bl), 69, 79(t), 84(tl), 107(m), 125(tm), 128-9; Alan Keohane, 68(bl); Ann Lambert, 125(m); Jenny Lamprell, 121(tl); Fiona Loader 37(ml), 39(t3); Simon Martin, 137(tm,tr); Thierry Mauger, 78-9, 80(t); Mr Mazrouie, 70(ml); Cathy Miller, 162(br); Patrick Miller, 73(ml), 139(bm); Anne Morgan, 10(t), (bl), 11(br), 13(tl), (m), 40(bl); Al Nakheel, 161(t,b); John Nowell, 18(ml), (mr); Donna Pepperdine 19(tr), 28(b), 42(t), 56(t), 67(tr); Peter Phelan (Arabian Wildlife Centre, Sharjah) 90(tr); Alan Pomering, 79(mr); Dr Anthony Preen, 130(tr,ml,mr); Rebecca Ridley, 50(t), 55(m), 97(tr,ml), 120(ml,bl), 142(tl); Moaz Sawaz, 96(ml,bl); Clara Semple 47(4); Shell, 154(m), 158-9(m), 159(tl); Adrian Sieberhagan, 93(bl); Dr Andrew Spalton, 89(bl); Sheila Unwin 66(br); Peter Upton 74-5, 74(t); Rhona Wells, 18(br).

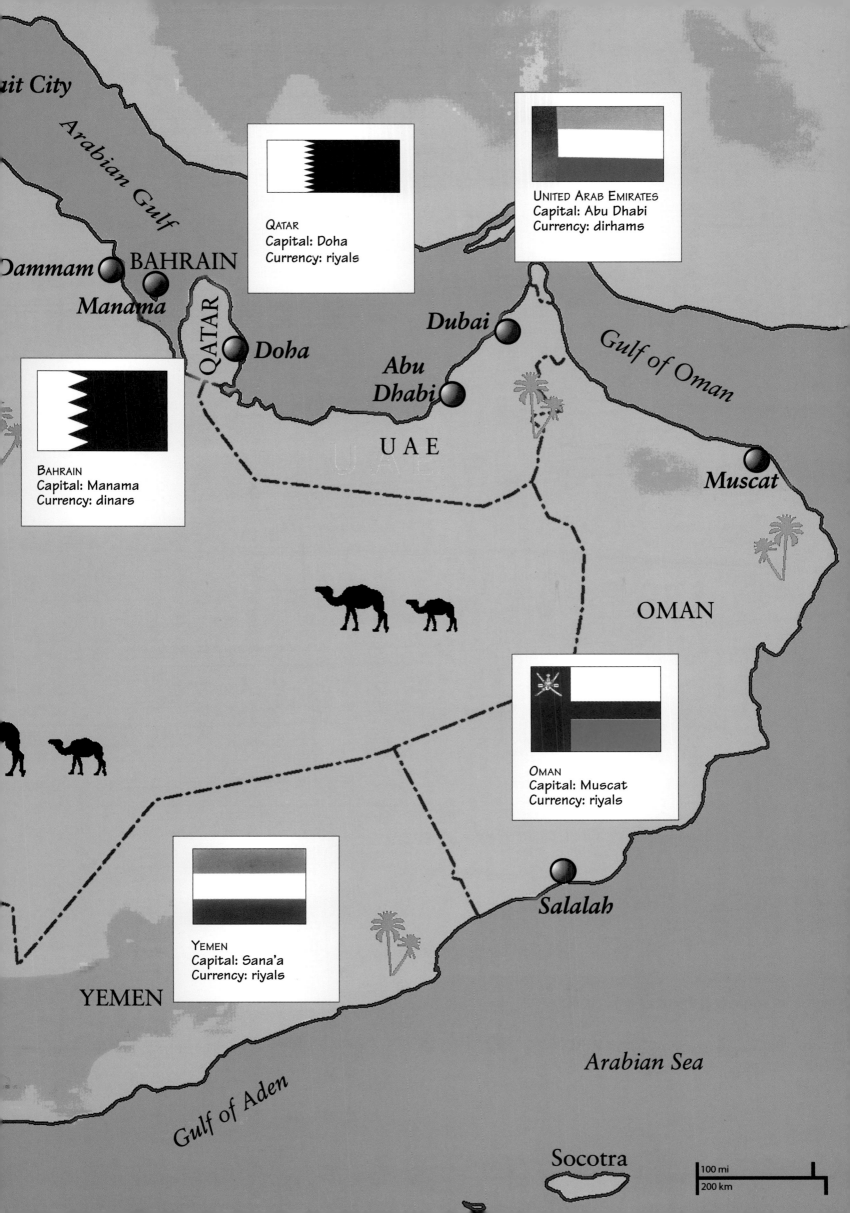

THE PAST

THE PAST

ARCHAEOLOGY — CLUES TO THE PAST

Archaeologists are scientists who study objects left behind from an ancient world. From these they build up a picture of how people lived thousands of years ago. Only a small number of the possessions used during a person's life survive over time. Natural materials, such as leather, decay. Wind and sand blowing across the land cause things to be buried and lost forever. The level of the ground builds up over many years so it must be removed in reverse order; the top layers first, working down to the bottom layers. When an ancient site is discovered, it must be treated with great care. Work on the site is called a dig and everything uncovered must be recorded and labelled in great detail. In the past, some unscrupulous people would remove things of value to add to their own collections or to sell.

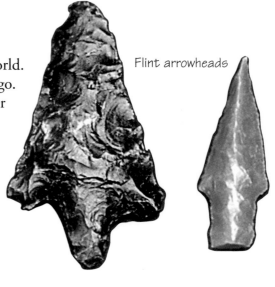

Flint arrowheads

Stone Age Tools

People are thought to have inhabited the Arabian peninsula for many thousands of years.

The first evidence of human activity comes from the Stone Age. Stone tools were hammered and shaped from rough stone.

They were probably finished by pressure flaking. Small flakes of stone were shaved off the surface with a sharpened rod.

An Egyptian tomb painting from 4,000 years ago shows how pressure flaking was done.

Pottery

One way archaeologists date sites is by studying pots found there. The style of pottery and the way it is decorated show the region it comes from and the period of time when it was made. Small pieces of pots are called potsherds, and have to be fitted together like the pieces of a jigsaw puzzle.

Rock Art Drawing

Rock art drawings are called petroglyphs.

The drawing of the animal (*above*) may have warned people about wild creatures living in the area.

A geometric sign like a circle has been drawn next to a man. It was a tribal sign. Petroglyphs are usually found at entrances to wadis. Perhaps they said who the area was owned by.

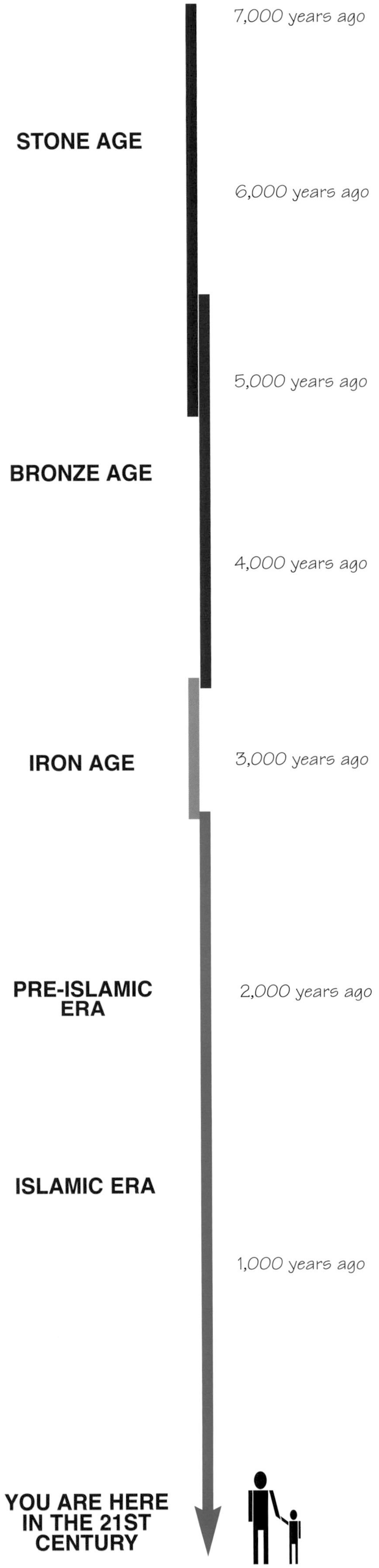

	7,000 years ago
STONE AGE	
	6,000 years ago
	5,000 years ago
BRONZE AGE	
	4,000 years ago
IRON AGE	3,000 years ago
PRE-ISLAMIC ERA	2,000 years ago
ISLAMIC ERA	
	1,000 years ago
YOU ARE HERE IN THE 21ST CENTURY	

A time line can help you see clearly the order of different periods of history discovered by the digs. You can also see approximately the length of time that each period lasted. However, the periods overlapped each other, gradually changing from one way of living to another.

When archaeologists work on a dig, they use all the objects found to date the site. They refer to a millennium or a name given to a period of time, such as the Bronze Age. Periods of history are often named after the material used then, like bronze.

A millennium is a 1,000 years.

?

How can we find out what people ate in the past?

Huge rubbish heaps of shells, called shell middens, have shown what types of shellfish were eaten. The same shells can be found on beaches today. The sea was a rich source of nourishment for early man. Fish bones and stone sinkers, used to weigh down nets, show that fishing was an important activity. Dugongs (*right*) also formed a large part of the diet of people living on the coast.

Dugong bones

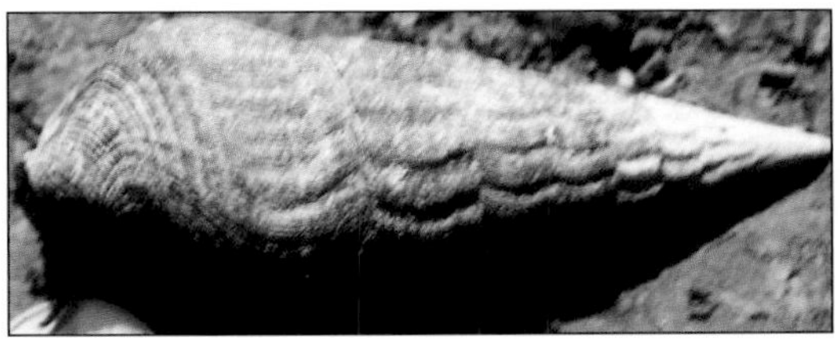

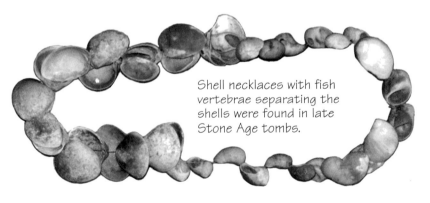

Shell necklaces with fish vertebrae separating the shells were found in late Stone Age tombs.

Skeletons

Research on bones and teeth gives information about the size of people, how they lived and the state of their health. Sometimes a skeleton will also reveal how the person died. Some of the skeletons unearthed in archaeological digs showed signs of violent death.

BRONZE AGE — TOMBS, A MIRROR OF LIFE

A bout 5,000 years ago, there was a big change in the way of life in the Arabian peninsula. The land called Magan, which is thought to have been in Oman and the mountainous area of the United Arab Emirates, was rich in copper ore. This copper provided the people with a material much sought after by their neighbours in Mesopotamia and the Indus Valley. There were advanced civilisations already established in these centres whose peoples sailed the waters of the Gulf trading their goods. Dilmun (modern day Bahrain) was an important port through which the ships passed. Trading copper with them produced great wealth for the people in the area and helped to create a culture known as *Umm an Nar*. Much of our knowledge about this period comes from the circular shaped tombs that were built near the settlements. The people who lived in those times believed in an afterlife. They buried their dead with all the precious and important items that had belonged to them during their lifetimes.

The Bronze Age

Relics of a furnace 40 cm high and 30 cm wide have been found in Oman. After crumbling the ore into small fragments with a stone, the ore had to be mixed with charcoal and put into a furnace. Bellows were used to blow air through the coals, and this brought the temperature up to 1,150°C. At this stage the melted copper was poured into a mould, formed from sand. After cooling, flat copper discs called ingots were obtained.

Copper bull's head found at Dilmun

The copper ore was smelted down to make weapons, fish hooks and ornaments. Copper was traded for textiles and hides.

Bronze Age weapons

Stone seals discovered at Dilmun (left) show trading activity took place more than 4,000 years ago.

Travellers came from Mesopotamia. They traded all the way along the coastline of the Gulf. Fragments of their painted pottery were found in settlements, alongside locally made pottery. Items were also found from the Indus Valley in Pakistan, then called Meluhha.

Map of the early sea routes along the Arabian Gulf

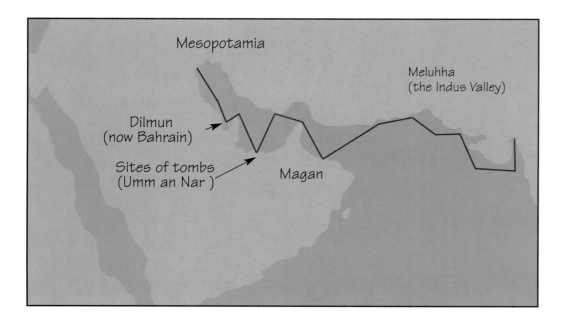

Mesopotamia

Dilmun (now Bahrain)

Sites of tombs (Umm an Nar)

Magan

Meluhha (the Indus Valley)

A fragment of painted pottery from Mesopotamia.

The Umm an Nar tombs

The *Umm an Nar* tombs were collective tombs, which meant that many people from the same family or tribe were buried together. The tombs were sealed up after each burial but re-opened when another death occurred. The number of people inside the tomb increased, sometimes reaching several hundred.

A reconstruction of an *Umm an Nar* tomb showing the chambers inside the tomb.

The tombs were large, measuring up to 14 metres in diameter, and were built with stones cut to shape. Inside the tombs were chambers where the bodies were laid. In some tombs there was evidence that, when the bodies had decomposed, the bones were burnt and put in another part of the tomb. The first of these tombs was discovered at *Umm an Nar*, near Abu Dhabi, in the United Arab Emirates. Other similar tombs, found in various areas of the Arabian peninsula, were named after *Umm an Nar*.

?

What jewellery might a person in an *Umm an Nar* tomb have worn?

An ivory comb from the Indus Valley.

All the objects may have been stored in a jewellery box carved from softstone.

Bracelets or necklaces carved from carnelian or clay beads.

A bronze ring

The bodies were discovered on their right side, in a bent position. The arms were either crossed over their chests or in front of their faces.

Nowadays people are buried in single graves, marked only with a small stone, and with no goods or possessions. Headstones mark graves in some parts of Arabia but are not commonly used.

Beehive-shaped tombs, found at Bat in Oman, were similar to the tombs of *Umm an Nar* but built earlier.

IRON AGE — VILLAGES AND FARMS

The Arabian peninsula is not a place of permanent drought but there is little rainfall. Before people were able to settle in large numbers and develop communities that depended on farming and agriculture, they had to understand how to control the water resources. During the Bronze Age, a system of wells, moats and canals was constructed. This was developed further during the Iron Age into the *falaj* system that is still used to distribute water today. The huge oases, where palm trees are cultivated, are only seen in the Middle East. Although water is naturally present under the ground, an oasis would not have developed in this way if man had not irrigated and tended the trees.

The village settlements of the Iron Age were built with mud bricks. The houses opened onto a big, enclosed courtyard and were built close together. A way of village life developed that can still be seen in farming areas today.

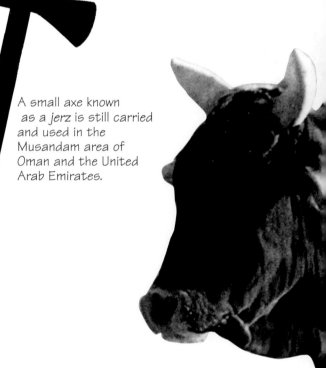

Different types of axe heads and hoes have been found in Iron Age settlements.

The development of a village

The first houses of mud bricks had only one room. These rooms were built as separate units where members of the same family lived. Each of the rooms was a few metres away from the next one.

Simple one-roomed stone houses with shelters made from palm fronds for the animals.

Pipes made out of clay were already being used for gutters to drain away the rain water.

Gradually, the houses grew larger with more rooms. Each room had its own use, such as the men's living quarters, the storage room and the kitchen.

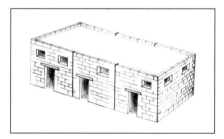

Larger houses with several rooms.

A small axe known as a jerz is still carried and used in the Musandam area of Oman and the United Arab Emirates.

By the Iron Age, houses built closely together formed a village.

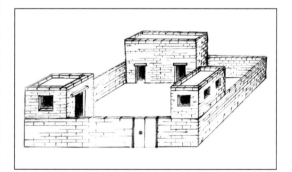

A courtyard was built around the house to enclose it.

Archaeologists have been able to work out how rooms were used from the different objects that were found in them. Almost everything known about village life comes from utensils that have been found.

Many pottery vessels were in use by the Iron Age.

The tradition of pottery has continued in many villages. Potters can still be seen working today.

What crops would a farmer in the Iron Age have grown?

Learning how to water the land so that crops could be grown all the year round was of the greatest importance to people living in Arabia. Dates have always been one of the most valuable sources of food in this area.

Crops were cultivated as food for man and animals. Three types of cereals were grown; wheat, oats and sorghum (right). Evidence comes from an imprint of a sorghum plant found in a mud brick.

Seeds of some fruits, such as watermelons, were found. It is not known whether vegetables were grown. All traces of vegetables tend to rot away as their seeds are not as large and hard as fruit and cereal seeds.

FACTOID

From archaeological digs we know farm animals would have included cows, sheep. goats and donkeys. It is not quite certain when camels were domesticated as the bones found may have been from wild camels and not farm ones.

Fodder for the animals was grown under the date palms. Bullocks were used to pull up water from the wells, and to plough fields. Donkeys were used to carry heavy loads. Stones for tethering the animals have been found as evidence that they were domesticated. In villages on the edge of the sandy and gravel plains, animals like goats and sheep were commonly kept in herds.

ANCIENT KINGDOMS

In the south-west corner of Arabia, now called Yemen, an advanced civilisation flourished 2,500 years ago. It was built on the huge wealth and prosperity earned from trade with the empires of Assyria, Egypt and later Rome. The countryside was the most fertile in the whole of the Arabian peninsula. High mountains caused rain to fall on these lands and they benefited from moisture brought by south-westerly monsoon winds as they swept over the Indian Ocean. Engineering technology was developed to control the rainwater with dams as it rushed into the wadis from the mountains. Wheat, barley and vegetables were grown. Hillsides were terraced to make use of every piece of ground. Ports on the coast were busy places. Arabian sailing skills were already advanced and luxurious goods were imported to supply the needs of the Romans and Egyptians. Some goods continued by boat through the Red Sea to the Mediterranean but others were packed onto camels to begin the long trek through the desert on what came to be known as 'the incense road'. The Arabian peninsula was such a rich and prosperous area that the Romans named it *Arabia Felix,* meaning 'happy' or 'blessed'. There were several kingdoms of which Saba, or Sheba, was the most powerful.

The Kingdom of Saba controlled the southern end of the incense road for more than a thousand years. One of Arabia's legendary characters, the Queen of Sheba, probably came from this Kingdom.

Frankincense tree

The visit of the Queen of Sheba to King Solomon in Jerusalem to discuss trade between their countries is recorded in the Koran. The Queen had a magical messenger, the hoopoe bird (*above*), which carried her messages to King Solomon.

Tall stone pillars standing in the desert today are believed to be part of the Queen of Sheba's palace.

?

Why were the people of Arabia described as 'the richest in the world'?

The Romans and Egyptians all had a taste for the luxurious goods imported from far away and carried in huge camel caravans to the Mediterranean and Syria. A caravan may have had as many as 3,000 camels in it. Frankincense, which was grown in Southern Arabia, was as valuable as gold or jewels. It was used in medicines and burnt in temples to help prayers reach heaven. We know the Egyptians used it for embalming corpses and pellets of it were found in Tutankhamen's tomb. The peak of Frankincense use was during the years of the Roman Empire, which nearly went bankrupt buying frankincense, while the Ancient Kingdoms of Arabia prospered.

Gradually there was less demand for incense and new routes were discovered to take goods from the east to the Mediterranean. The 1,000 year old civilization came to an end and many people emigrated to other parts of the Arabian peninsula.

The northern end of the incense road was controlled by the Nabataeans. The beautiful city of Petra was their capital and was built on taxes extracted from merchants travelling the incense road. The city of Hijr (*above*), now called Madain Saleh, in Saudi Arabia was also an important centre of trade.

Arts flourished in the region, and one of the earliest written languages recorded the devotion of the people to their many gods. They worshipped astral bodies – the Sun, the Moon and Venus, which they called the Morning Moon.

Can computers help us find out about life thousands of years ago?

Yes, by feeding data about the size and shape of ancient buildings into a computer it will produce a model of how that building would have looked. A team of archaeologists working in the Yemen fed data about a temple, built for the moon god Almaqah, nearly 3,000 years ago into a computer programme. Just using a set of facts and figures the computer came up with this design of a temple with high stone pillars leading into three huge chambers.

These neatly incised geometric characters are from an early script developed in southern Arabia. Samples of similar script found in Oman, Saudi Arabia and the United Arab Emirates are evidence of journeys made by the incense traders.

FACTOID

Out of their wealth the kings of the ancient kingdoms built huge irrigation dams. Much rain fell during the monsoons, which occurred twice a year. Roaring masses of water rushed down the mountain sides. This water had to be contained so it could be funnelled onto farming land as it was needed. A huge dam was built at Marib.

16 metres high and 600 metres long a dam built at Marib in Southern Yemen was a huge technological achievement and was called 'the 8th wonder of the world'. It is believed to have held up 150,000 cubic metres of water. Between 25,000 and 50,000 people of Saba lived on the food grown in the fields it irrigated.

The Marib dam collapsed in the fifth century AD although attempts were made to keep it going for quite some time afterwards. It was certainly a great technological achievement, and has now been rebuilt by Sheikh Zayed, ruler of the United Arab Emirates.

Some remains of the original damn still stand. Shown here (*right*) is the southern sluice of the old Marib dam.

THE INCENSE ROAD — FRANKINCENSE

The best frankincense comes from trees that grow in southern Arabia and Oman. In the past medicines were made from it and as its fragrant smoke drifted upwards it was thought to give protection from 'the evil eye'. Collecting the resin that comes from frankincense trees is difficult work and in ancient times it was shrouded in mystery. Herodotus, a Greek writer, told of winged serpents that guarded the trees. What is certain is that there were many dangers and perils on the 2,735 kilometre journey as it was carried across the Arabian peninsula. Hundreds of camels laden with goods travelled the route with their masters. City states along the incense road grew rich supplying the needs of the camel caravans and charging them taxes as they went through. There were severe punishments if they departed from the road; so taxes could not be avoided. Frankincense was a very expensive necessity at that time and brought great wealth to everyone dealing in it.

Herodotus told of winged serpents that guarded the frankincense trees.

In March, April and May the bark of the tree is cut, and tiny droplets of frankincense ooze out and solidify. The tree must be at least three to four years old, and it is important to cut the bark to exactly the right depth.

The freshly harvested gum resin is sorted into different varieties of frankincense, according to its shade. The light pastel shades are the best, while the darker shades are not worth so much. It is packed into 40 kg. sacks to be sold in the souqs. The resin is not usually burnt on its own. It is ground into a fine powder and mixed with other fragrant ingredients to make a product called *bokhur*, which is burnt along with chips of oud wood to perfume a house.

A great port, Khor Ruri, was built in southern Oman to export the frankincense. It was guarded by the city of Samharam.

Globules of frankincense ooze from skilfully made incisions.

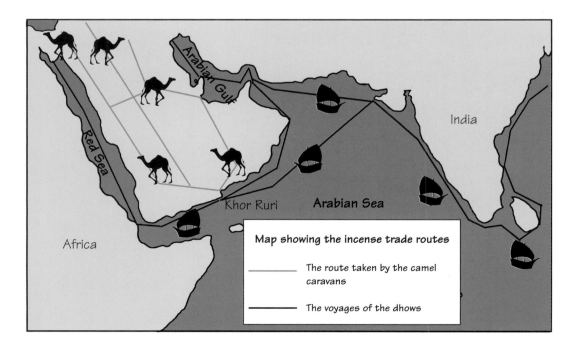

Map showing the incense trade routes

_____ The route taken by the camel caravans

———— The voyages of the dhows

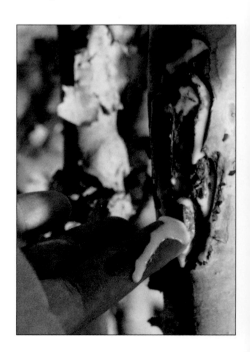

Does frankincense still cost a lot of money?

Shops in the souqs of Arabia are chock-a-block with sacks of frankincense and myrrh, perfumes and incense burners along with other traditional goods. Both the frankincense resin and the ground-up version, called *bokhur*, are very reasonably pr ced today. Although still burnt regularly in Arabia, the amounts that are harvested are small compared with its peak in Roman times.

Artefacts from southern Arabia and the countries of the Mediterranean have been discovered in archaeological sites throughout the Arabian peninsula. They plot the journey taken by the caravaners and show what items were traded for the valuable goods they carried.

Traditional pottery frankincense burners are still made in Dhofar, Oman. These brightly decorated burners are known to have been made for several hundreds of years in this area.

Glass from Rome

Amphorae from Greece

Examples of incense burners.

The prosperous trading routes brought about the use of money to Arabia

Many different coinages in silver circulated throughout the Arabian peninsula. Some coins were minted in southern Arabia using their own designs but city states in eastern Arabia copied coins imported along the trade routes. Designs from Greek coins were frequently used.

Coins with the goddess of Athena on one side and the owl on the reverse were minted locally.

The smallest coin was called a drachm and weighed about four grams.

A tetradrachm was four times the weight of the drachm. This coin weighed 15.6 grams. It had the head of the god Herekles on the front of the coin and Zeus on the back. Zeus has a horse on the palm of his hand.

THE BIRTH OF ISLAM

Islam is an Arabic word, meaning peace and submission to God's will. People who believe in Islam are called Muslims and they accept the teachings of God (*Allah*) as revealed to the Prophet Mohammed, who was born around AD 570 in Makkah. His parents died when he was young, so he grew up poor and illiterate. When he was eight, he went to live with his uncle, Abu Talib, who was a merchant. Mohammed started working as a shepherd. At the age of twenty-five he married Khadijah, a rich widow, and for many years he travelled the desert buying and selling goods. He gained a reputation as an honest and learned man. When he was forty, Mohammed received his first message from God. The revelations were in Arabic and Mohammed memorized them.

As Muslims pray, they use the three divisions of their finger joints to count the number of prayers they have said. Sometimes prayer beads are used instead to aid their memory when praying. The beads come in strings with 33 or 99 beads on them.

The Five Pillars of Islam

Muslims accept these duties:

Shahada
To believe that Allah is the one true God and that Mohammed is the last prophet.

Salah
To pray five times a day facing Makkah.

Sawn
To fast between sunrise and sunset during the Holy Month of Ramadan.

Zakat
To give charity to the poor.

Hajj
To make a pilgrimage to Makkah at least once during their lifetime.

Mohammed asked his scribes to write down the words that God revealed to him over 23 years of his life. This record is the Koran (*Qur'an*). It instructs Muslims in what they must and must not do to gain their reward on the Day of Judgment.

The Holy Koran is written in classical Arabic. Arabic calligraphers create beautiful works of art from the words of the Koran.

Ramadan
The Holy Month of *Ramadan* is a very special time of prayer in the Muslim year. Fasting takes place during daylight hours.

At the end of the month, *Eid Al Fitr* is celebrated. Families traditionally meet together for a meal. Nowadays, many people travel long distances to be with their families on this occasion.

A moon sighting committee is set up to look for the new moon that announces the start of the Holy Month.

Calls to prayer can be heard loudly and clearly five times a day from minarets of mosques across the land.

Why is the Islamic calendar different from the calendar used in Western countries (the Gregorian calendar?)

In the year AD 622 an important event occurred in the life of the Prophet Mohammed. After the revelation of the Koran from God, he preached to a group of Muslim followers in Makkah, but his reputation quickly spread beyond this city. Mohammed was critical of the behaviour of the powerful Qurayshi rulers of Makkah, and he particularly spoke out against their worship of idols. Eventually his followers were vindictively persecuted. They could take no more suffering, and Mohammed's life was in danger, so they migrated to the nearby town of Yathrib, where they were welcomed. This event is called the Hijra and marks both the start of Year 1 of the Islamic calendar and the formation of the new Islamic State. Yathrib, where the practice of Islam began to unfold without restriction, became known as al-Madina al Muawwara – the City of Light.

FACTOID

!

There are only 354 days in a year!

The Islamic calendar is lunar, which means governed by the moon. It is about 11 days shorter than the Western calendar. Each numbered year is followed by either H or AH, being the initial letters of the Latin name 'Anno Hegirae' – in the year of the Hijra.

Islamic year within Gregorian year		
Islamic	Gregorian	Difference
1228	1813	585
1261	1845	584
1295	1878	583
1329	1911	583
1362	1943	581
1396	1976	580
1429	2008	570
1463	2041	578
1496	2073	577
1530	2106	576
1564	2139	575

Makkah is the most sacred city in Islam. It is where the Prophet Mohammed was born, and where he started preaching God's word. It is the site of the Hajj pilgrimage which all Muslims must make during their lifetime.

The black cloth covering the *Ka'bah* is called the *Kiswah*. The *Kiswah* is replaced every year by a new one which takes teams of weavers and embroiderers a full year to make.

The Ka'bah
Pilgrims visit the Great Mosque in Makkah (*above*) which contains the *Ka'bah*, a cubical stone building 45 metres high. According to the Koran, the first *Ka'bah* was built by the Prophet Ibrahim (Abraham) and his son Ismai'il as a place of worship of the one God. The *Ka'bah* is the point that Muslims face in their daily prayers.

Pilgrims on the Hajj change their usual everyday clothes for a simple white seamless garment, the *ihram*. For men the *ihram* consists of two lengths of white material, one covering the body from waist to below the knee, the other thrown over the shoulder. For women it is a simple white gown.

THE SPREAD OF ISLAM

God's instruction to the Prophet Mohammed was to spread the word of Islam far and wide. The rapid rise of Islam in the 7th century transformed the history of Arabia. By AD 630, the Prophet had converted the people of Makkah, and he returned there from Madinah. By the year of his death in AD 632, tribes from distant regions recognised him as the senior ruler of the Arabian peninsula, helping unite them for the first time. He was their political and military leader as well as their religious leader. The death of the Prophet Mohammed presented the small Muslim community with a serious problem: who was to follow him as its leader? This was solved by the selection of a Caliph – which means 'successor'. Caliph became the name given to the ruler of each Islamic community, known as **Caliphates**. His successors shared a vast empire which stretched from the Atlantic Ocean to the borders of India.

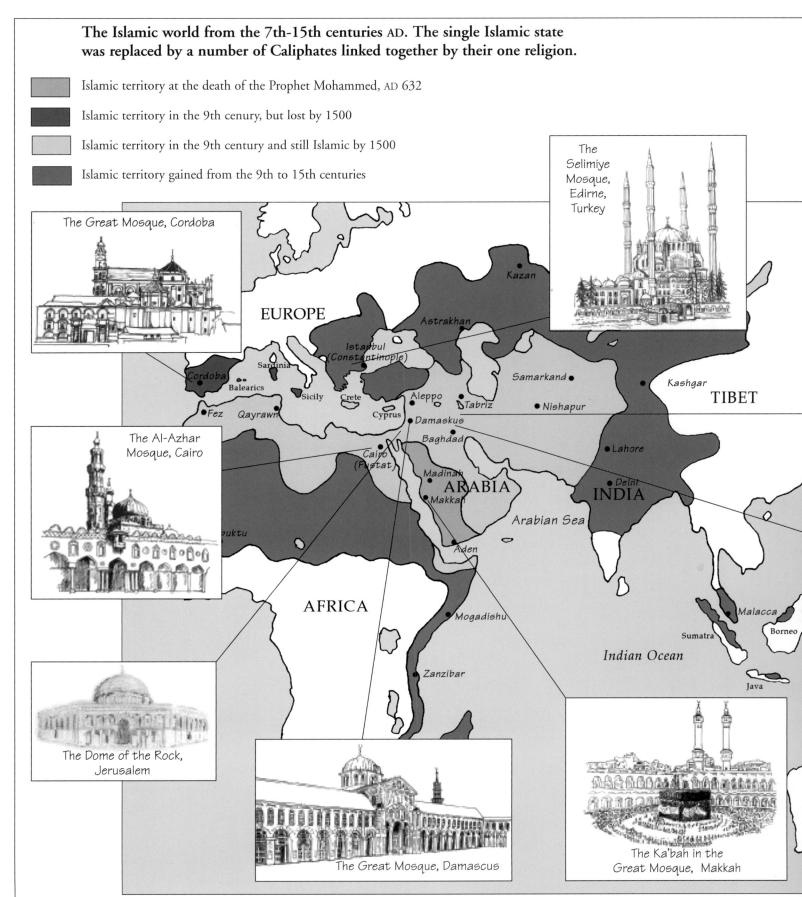

The Islamic world from the 7th-15th centuries AD. The single Islamic state was replaced by a number of Caliphates linked together by their one religion.

- Islamic territory at the death of the Prophet Mohammed, AD 632
- Islamic territory in the 9th cenury, but lost by 1500
- Islamic territory in the 9th century and still Islamic by 1500
- Islamic territory gained from the 9th to 15th centuries

The Selimiye Mosque, Edirne, Turkey

The Great Mosque, Cordoba

The Al-Azhar Mosque, Cairo

The Dome of the Rock, Jerusalem

The Great Mosque, Damascus

The Ka'bah in the Great Mosque, Makkah

EUROPE

Kazan

Astrakhan

Istanbul (Constantinople)

Sardinia

Cordoba

Balearics

Sicily

Crete

Cyprus

Samarkand

Kashgar

TIBET

Fez

Qayrawn

Aleppo

Tabriz

Nishapur

Damaskus

Baghdad

Lahore

Cairo (Fustat)

Madinah

Delhi

INDIA

ARABIA

Makkah

Arabian Sea

uktu

Aden

AFRICA

Mogadishu

Malacca

Sumatra

Borneo

Indian Ocean

Zanzibar

Java

The airlines of Arabia display a special rotating symbol which always points to Makkah to assist Muslim travellers. It is important that they know the direction of Makkah when they kneel to pray.

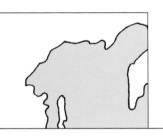

The Shah Mosque, Isfahan

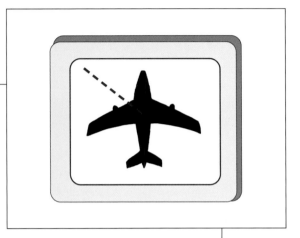

The minaret, Samarra, Iraq

USTRALIA

FACTOID

Over one billion Muslims now worship in every corner of the globe. The largest group of Muslims live in Indonesia, but there are also large numbers in Europe, the United States of America, China and Asia.

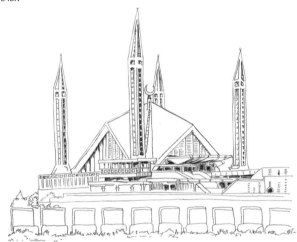

The Shah Faisal Mosque in Islamabad, Pakistan, is built in a strikingly modern style while keeping the traditional parts of mosque design.

Damascus – Capital of a new Empire

In AD 661 the governor of Syria, Mu'awiya Ibn Abi Sufyan, became Caliph of the Islamic State and moved its centre from Madinah to Damascus in Syria.

Damascus, the Umayyad capital city, was one of the most ancient and prosperous cities in the Middle East.

The picture shows the imposing minaret of the city's Umayyad Mosque.

Damascus is thought to be the oldest continuously inhabited city in the world.

In AD 750 the Umayyad caliphate was overthrown by the rival Abbasid clan who established their own caliphate in Iraq. They eventually settled their capital in Baghdad which became the hub of international trade and learning. Under the Abbasids, Islamic civilisation achieved its golden age in the fields of science, medicine and philosophy.

What was the job of a Caliph?

A Caliph was expected to lead the community according to the Koran, and the practice of the Prophet. His role was to uphold and spread the new faith, to promote the well-being of Muslims and to rule his state wisely. However, as the Islamic Empire grew, the Caliphs had to pay more attention to the practical problems of government.

Many local rulers throughout Islamic history also claimed to be Caliphs, but they were not recognised outside their part of the Empire.

MASTERS OF THE SEA

From earliest times, there has been a great tradition of seafaring in the Arab world. More than twelve hundred years ago the longest route being sailed by mankind, from the Gulf to China, was being made in Arabian ships. It was a remarkable achievement. Arabian mariners also developed the lateen sail that made more efficient use of wind than the earlier square sail. They timed the departure of their voyages to make use of monsoon winds blowing across the Indian Ocean. Early seafarers seldom made journeys out of sight of land, although they went great distances going from one port to the next. Sea voyages were full of hardship. Disasters often overtook the sailors. Treacherous rocks and reefs, shallow sandbanks and violent storms were hazards to be overcome. Swift boats rowed by pirates dashed out from hidden harbours to steal their cargoes. Stories and legends were woven around the bravery and skills of the seafarers who returned home safely from their travels. They were the superheroes of their time.

Natural landmarks, such as mountains, helped early seafarers to navigate. Sightings of seabirds or sea-snakes were evidence of land nearby.

Although no pictures exist of very early Arabian boats, scholars have studied evidence of the way they were constructed and the materials they were made from. They have described the way boats probably looked.

The hulls were double-ended, coming to a point at both bow and stern.

The wood used to make the hull was teak or other hards woods imported from India. The planks were stitched together with rope made from the fibres of coconut husks.

Coconut fibres were soaked in water.

The fibres were thrashed until they became stringy. Then they were twisted to make cords.

The planks were sewn together with stitches of cord. The cord was threaded through holes drilled along the edges of the planks.

The planks were coated in fish-oil to seal them from the harmful effects of seawater. Shark oil was said to be the best.

Originally anchors were made from large stones with a hole in the centre through which ropes were attached. They were later replaced by metal anchors.

The mast was very high. This was a big problem during storms. It was sometimes cut off and thrown overboard so the ship did not capsize.

Sails were woven from leaves of the coconut palm. Cotton sailcloth was also used. The sails were attached to a long spar which was nearly the whole length of the boat. It was difficult to move the sails to the other side of the mast when the ship changed direction.

The boat was steered by a large oar hung over the side which acted as a rudder. The side rudder was later replaced by one on the stern of the boat.

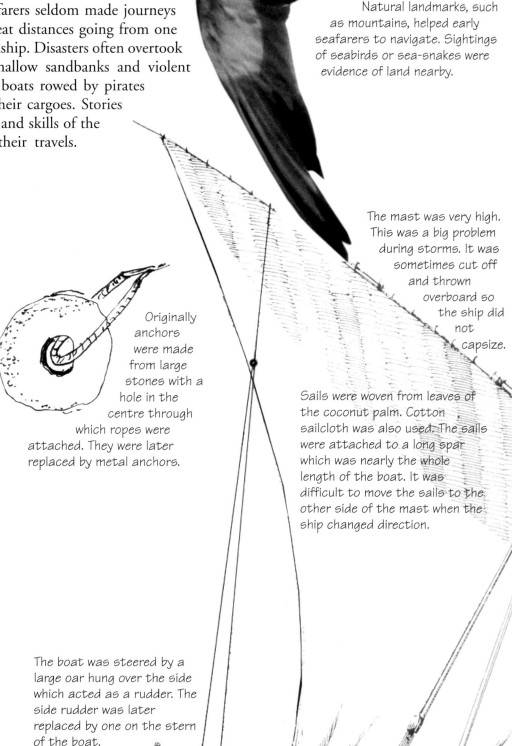

Development of the Lateen Sail

In the ancient world the square sail was used in ships from the Mediterranean to Northern Europe. It worked well to keep the ship stable in rough seas.

On the Nile in Egypt a lugsail was used. The square sail was set at an angle from the bow to the stern, known as 'fore and aft'. It made use of wind coming from the side of the boat.

A further development was to shorten the front of the sail and heighten it at the back. This resulted in the sail known as the 'lateen', which was used in Arabian waters. This shape proved the most effective for sailing close to the wind.

?

Why did sailing ships have to stay in port for much of the year?

Sailors waited in ports, sometimes for months at a time, for the direction of the monsoon winds to change. The south-west monsoon carried the ships to India. The north-east monsoon would bring them back to Arabian shores. It would also take ships down the east coast of Africa.

NORTH-EAST MONSOON
blew from October to March

N

SOUTH-WEST MONSOON
blew from April to October

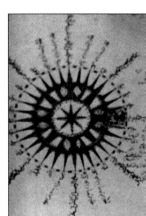

?

Fact or Fiction?

Was Sindbad the Sailor a real person – or was he made up?

A collection of traditional stories called *The Thousand and One Nights* tells of Sindbad who survived seven voyages. During each one he encountered incredible creatures.

It is claimed that Sindbad came from the port of Sohar, in Oman. Sohar was a large trading centre at the time the stories were written. Although it is not known whether Sindbad ever existed, his stories were based on the real adventures of Arab sea-farers.

Sindbad meets a bird of immense size called 'the rukh' which feeds its babies on elephants.

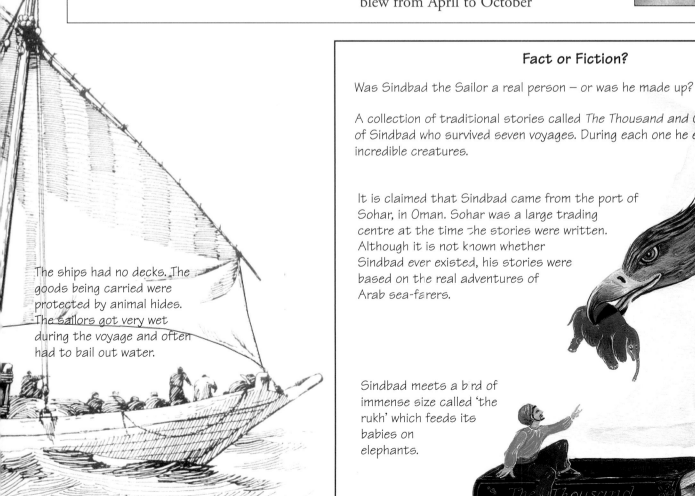

The ships had no decks. The goods being carried were protected by animal hides. The sailors got very wet during the voyage and often had to bail out water.

THE GOLDEN AGE OF SAIL

Boat building, navigating and knowledge of the sea were essential skills passed down from one generation to the next in the Arab world. During the 9th century AD, 1,200 years ago, a golden age of seafaring began and this was to last for many centuries. Merchants financed voyages to Africa and countries to the east of Arabia in search of riches. They bought places for themselves and their servants on a ship and set sail in the care of an experienced shipmaster know as a *nakhuda*. Assisted by his crew, the *nakhuda* guided the boat to far-away destinations. They reached their home port many months later, loaded with precious cargoes and thanking God for their safe return. The merchant sold the cargo while the crew repaired the boat and made ready for the next voyage. The seafaring knowledge of these times was not improved on for hundreds of years.

The night sky in Arabia is always clear and bright making it easy to see stars well. Here the Haley Bop comet is clearly visible.

?

How was it possible to navigate without a compass?

Finding their way across the oceans was a problem for early seafarers. Travellers trekking by camel across the vast empty deserts of the Arabian peninsula shared the same problem. The science of astronomy, knowledge of the stars, gave an answer. The direction in which they travelled could be worked out by the rising and setting of the stars. They believed that God had placed the stars to guide them in the darkness of the land and sea.

As the earth rotates, the constellations move their position. The Pole star, also known as the North star or Polaris, is unusual in that it always lies north of anyone observing it. At the time of the first Arab explorers the Pole star did not exactly mark the North Pole, due to the slight wobbling of earth on its axis and the relatively slow movement of the stars. However, a fainter star which is more accurate was probably known to them.

Movement of the stars during a typical night.

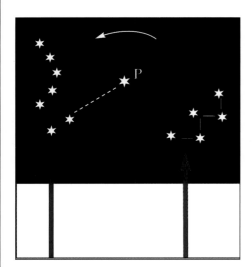

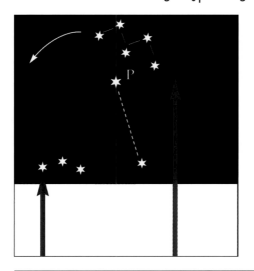

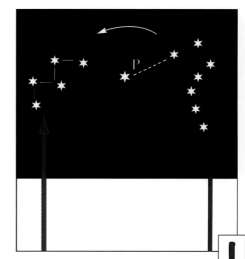

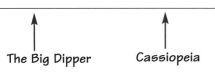

The Big Dipper   Cassiopeia

The Big Dipper and Cassiopeia are shown with the Pole Star between them. Although the Big Dipper and Cassiopeia move during the night the Pole Star remains in the same position.

The height of the Pole star was calculated to find the latitude of the ship and the port to which it was heading.

!

FACTOID

A small piece of wood only 5 cms long, with a piece of knotted string going through the middle, was all that was needed to plot the latitude of the ship. Called a *kamal*, it was held out at arm's length with the string pulled tight. Using the width of his fingers to measure, the sailor held the bottom edge of the wood on the horizon and calculated the number of finger widths to the Pole star. Fifty-six finger widths were equal to 90 degrees.

The knowledge of navigators was written in books called *rahmanis*. They gave clear and detailed instructions about the sea, anchorages, winds, currents, the stars and latitudes of different ports. The highest grade of navigator was called a *mu'allim*.

Ahmad ibn-Majid, born in Julfar, near Ras al Khaimah, was a *mu'allim* at the end of the 15th century. He became one of the most famous navigators in the history of seamanship.

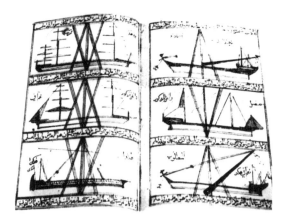

A manuscript in the Rahmani tradition preserved at Muscat, Oman.

Ahmad ibn-Majid wrote a *rahmani* called the *Book of Profitable Things Concerning The First Principle and Rules of Navigation*. It gave such valuable instructions, particularly about the Red Sea and the Indian Ocean, that his fame spread far and wide. The Portuguese explorer Vasco da Gama is said to have sought his help in crossing the Indian Ocean. Some historians have disputed this. Evidence now points to another pilot, who was more likely to have given the Portuguese this information than Ahmad ibn-Majid. The arrival of the Portuguese was a disastrous event for the Arab world.

?

What were the luxury goods that people traded?

From Africa

1. Ivory
2. Ostrich feathers
3. Leopard skins
4. Tortoiseshell

From the East

5. Porcelain
6. Bamboo
7. Teak
8. Oils for perfumes and incense
9. Silk

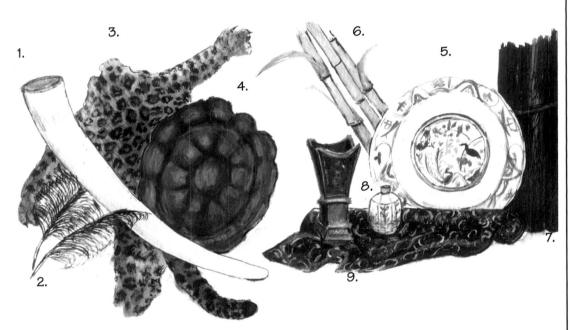

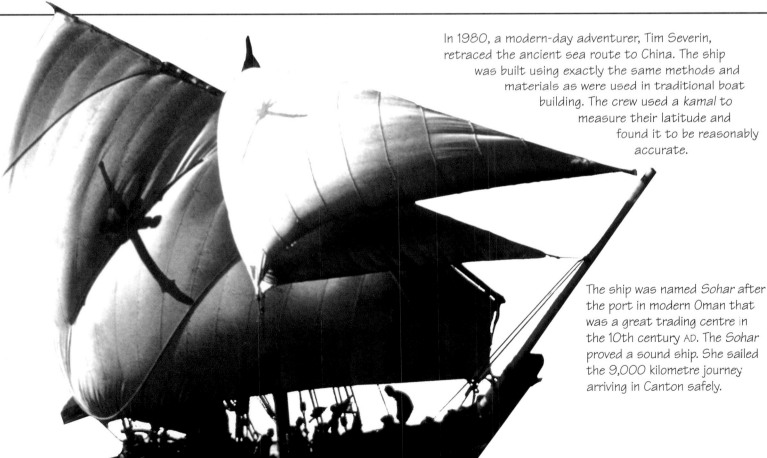

In 1980, a modern-day adventurer, Tim Severin, retraced the ancient sea route to China. The ship was built using exactly the same methods and materials as were used in traditional boat building. The crew used a *kamal* to measure their latitude and found it to be reasonably accurate.

The ship was named *Sohar* after the port in modern Oman that was a great trading centre in the 10th century AD. The *Sohar* proved a sound ship. She sailed the 9,000 kilometre journey arriving in Canton safely.

THE SPICE TRADE AND THE PORTUGUESE

The word 'spice' comes from the Latin *species* and means an item of special value. To the Europeans spices were an exotic commodity which only grew in tropical eastern lands. They had to be transported over thousands of kilometres of ocean and were in great demand both for flavouring foods and for use in medicines. Spices became the main reason for trade on a huge scale between India, Africa and the Arabian peninsula. The spice trade brought power, influence and wealth to the people who controlled it. From ports on the southern coast of Arabia, ships loaded with spices sailed through the Red Sea or the Arabian Gulf on their journey to Europe. After a short overland trek via the cities of Petra in Jordan or Palmyra in Syria the spices reached the European marketplaces. The ports of Venice and Genoa in Italy became exceedingly wealthy as a result of this trade. Great rivalry developed between them and other European trading nations. This resulted in Vasco da Gama, a Portuguese sea captain, setting sail in 1498 to find an alternative route round the southern tip of Africa to the lands where the spices grew. His success led to a new era in the history of Arabia.

The Strait of Hormuz guard the narrow entrance to the Gulf

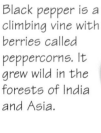

Which spices were most sought after

When Vasco da Gama returned to Portugal in 1499 he brought with him a cargo of cinnamon, cloves, ginger and pepper.

Cinnamon is the dried bark of the cinnamon tree. The first cinnamon trees were native to Sri Lanka.

Ginger is the stem of the ginger plant which grows underground. It originally grew in India and Asia.

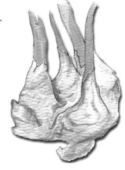

Black pepper is a climbing vine with berries called peppercorns. It grew wild in the forests of India and Asia.

Cloves are the dried flower buds of the clove tree which was native to Indonesia. The small island of Pemba off the coast of East Africa was also famous for its cloves.

Spices were shipped through the Red Sea and the Arabian Gulf. The wealthy city state of Hormuz controlled the route through the Gulf and collected taxes from traders using it. Ports on the coast also flourished through trade and local agriculture.

Spices were used to hide unpleasant household smells and mask the taste of food that was often far from fresh. They were also renowned for their healing properties.

A huge selection of spices is still sold from sacks in the spice souqs.

In 1506 the Portuguese fleet, led by Afonso de Albuquerque, arrived in the town of Muscat having first captured the island of Socotra, which gave them a base to control the spice route through the Red Sea.

Many sea battles were fought between the Portuguese and the people from Hormuz but the city eventually fell to the invaders. All the towns along the east coast from Ras al Khaimah in the north, to Quryiat in the south, were drawn into the battles. The Portuguese held control of the Gulf and Indian Ocean for about a hundred years. Local ships had to obtain passes from the Portuguese permitting them to trade.

The two massive forts of Miran and Jalali were built by the Portuguese to defend the harbour at Muscat. Fort Mirani was the first Omani fort to be fitted with cannons. Several other forts were built by them along the coast and one, already in existence in Bahrain, was rebuilt so that cannons could be used to defend it.

Changes brought about by the Portuguese

The arrival of cannons and gunpowder was to alter the nature of war in the area. From this time onwards they became essential items of attack and defence.
Architectural design of forts changed to accommodate the cannons and make best use of cannonfire as a defence.

On Portuguese boats the shape of the stern was square. This square stern replaced the traditional pointed shape of some Arab boats after this date. Pearling boats, called jalibuts, are an example of square sterns.

The traditional way of making the hull of a boat by sewing planks of wood together came to an end. The Portuguese boats were more strongly constructed using iron nails. This method was adopted by Arab shipbuilders. In 1650 the Portuguese were eventually expelled from the area by the Omani navy. Dutch, British and French ships quickly arrived in Arabian waters after the Portuguese left, anxious to take part in trade from the east.

Afonso de Albuquerque

Jalali Fort in Muscat

IONAL

TRADITIONAL
LIFE

TRADITIONAL BUILDING MATERIALS

Structures are any kind of building put up by man. The buildings serve a variety of purposes, depending on needs of the people living in the community. In the past, people had only local materials that were easily available to them when they constructed their buildings. However, they used these materials to the best advantage, creating buildings that were well suited to the climate. Without modern transport, collecting materials for building was a time-consuming task. The materials available on the sandy coast were coral stone dug from the seabed, gypsum (known as *juss*) or parts of the palm tree. Some houses were built entirely from palm fronds. In winter, the palm frond houses, known as *areesh*, were made warmer and windproof by using extra leaves to increase the thickness of the walls. The trunk of the palm tree provided wood but it was soft. Hard wood was generally in short supply. Poles of mangrove branches were used, but often wood had to be brought from overseas and was expensive. In mountainous areas, stone and clay were also available as building materials.

In the Yemen, traditional materials are used to build thatched huts in lowland areas. Roofs are made from reeds or the hard dry foliage of the *gadab* bush.

A house built from the complete palm frond, called *sa'af* in Arabic, was cool in summer. The fronds were tied together with coir strings made from fibres of the tree. Panels called *da'an* were used to construct walls. Animal enclosures were also made from palm fronds.

Although palm frond houses were usually very strong, a shamal wind or a swarm of locusts could destroy them.

Many buildings clearly show pieces of coral embedded into gypsum (below). The white powder-like gypsum (or *juss*) was limestone that had to be fired in an oven before being ground into powder and mixed with water into a plaster-like consistency.

Mud was widely used for making bricks. Straw was mixed with the mud (right) and shaped with wooden moulds into bricks. Sometimes the mud was rolled out flat on the ground and cut into squares. The bricks were either sun-dried or fired in a large oven.

FACTOID

Mud-bricks are still made in Yemen where sky-scrapers, constructed entirely of mud, show what a strong building material it can be.

'The Manhattan of the Desert' is the term used to describe the mud-brick town of Shibam.

Wth 500 houses built seven or eight storeys high, it became a UNESCO World Heritage site in 1982.

The skyline of coastal cities on sandy shores was low. A second storey was sometimes added to a house to provide a living area cooled by breezes from the sea in hot summer months. There was plenty of space so it was not neccesary to make taller buildings and it was hard work collecting materials for construction.

In mountain areas, stone was used as a building material. In some areas 'dry stone walling' was constructed by placing large stones on top of each other with the cracks filled in by smaller stones. In other areas traditional cement called sarouj was used to fill the cracks. Sarouj was also used to complete a wall by covering the entire surface with it.

Which materials make the strongest buildings?

Walls of watchtowers and forts were built for strength. Some watchtowers had a stone and mortar base with a mud-brick top. Others were constructed solely from mud brick. Sometimes the base was filled with rubble for extra strength with the entrance to the lower floor at first floor level. A ladder was placed up to the door, and pulled inside the tower when villagers were safely inside.

ISLAMIC ARCHITECTURE – HOUSES

When we look at traditional architecture of a country we have a picture of the life of the people who lived there. The houses they lived in, the mosques where they worshipped and the market places where they traded their goods show us the pattern of their daily lives. The forts and watchtowers remind us that they had to defend their towns.

Although the Arabian peninsula has many different countries, each with its own original style of building, the architecture is similar in many ways. Islam is the religion of the whole area. People go to the mosque to worship and they like privacy in their homes. The climate is similar in all the countries. The design and decoration of buildings continue today to follow traditions used throughout the Arab world, known as Islamic architecture.

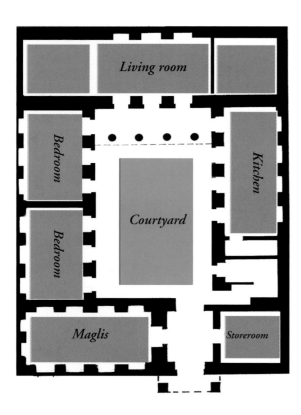

The Layout

Privacy is important in Islam. Houses have small windows often covered with a decorative wooden grill (*mashrabiyya*). This enables women inside to look out without being seen themselves, working in the same way as a net curtain.

Rooms face into a central courtyard, with separate quarters for men and women. Each room has its own purpose and it is not possible to walk from one room to the next.

A wall surrounds the courtyard with only one door leading to the world outside. The doors are a feature of the architecture; often beautifully carved from wood or colourfully decorated metal.

How are windtowers used to air-condition houses?

Windtowers are built on two-storey buildings and rise about fifteen metres above the ground. Examples of windtower houses can be seen throughout the Gulf from Kuwait to Ras al Khaimah and the Musandam. As well as being family homes, the houses stored dates, grain and other goods.

The barjeel, the wind-catcher (left), is a four sided structure that funnels the breeze from any direction down to the lower floor of the house below, cooling it.

The barjeel allows cold air to enter the tower through vents. Hot air in the room below rises above colder air and so is passed out of the house. It is a very efficient form of air conditioning.

Above, a traditional residence in Jeddah, Saudi Arabia.

Decorative screens on the windows made from pierced gypsum allow air to circulate round the room. Thick walls also help to keep buildings cool.

In places where there is heavy rainfall, such as the mountainous Abha area, clay bricks have horizontal slabs of stone inserted between the layers of bricks to break up the flow of water across the surface.

Every house contains a *majlis*, like that below, where men of the family meet to entertain guests and discuss affairs of the day. Cushioned seating is arranged on carpets around the edge of the room. Rulers hold regular meetings in the *majlis* where they listen to opinions and requests from the community.

Stone and brick townhouses in Yemen (*above*) are world famous for their unique building styles. Some of them are 500 years old. The lower storeys of the houses are built of stone, and the upper floors of fired bricks. Decorative white limestone on window surrounds was traditionally used by pilgrims returning from Makkah, white being a sacred colour. It is also thought to attract the light and keep out flies.

Inside the house, windows and ceilings are often decorated with shapes inspired by nature such as flowers or leaves.

In Saudi Arabia unfired clay bricks, covered with plaster, are used to make houses with mouldings, crennellations and parapets. Windows and peepholes, where visitors can be viewed, are part of the design.

ISLAMIC ARCHITECTURE — MOSQUES

Mosques are holy places of worship and learning. They are centres of community life and every district has its own mosque. The Prophet Mohammed built a mosque in Madinah of simple, unbaked bricks with a roof of palm fronds, facing into a courtyard where his followers came to pray and listen to him speak. The site of a mosque was considered to be sacred and when an old mosque collapsed another one would be built on the same site. Today there are many different styles of mosques. It is usual to see domes and minarets on the outside of a mosque built around a courtyard. The first words of the Koran which were revealed to the Prophet Mohammed are 'Read in the name of your Lord'. In the past, the only schooling children received took place in mosques.

The Al Khamis mosque (*left*) in Bahrain is one of the oldest in the Gulf. The date of its original construction is not known for certain, but is thought to be about 1,200 years old.

The Call to Prayer

Allah is the greatest
I bear witness that there is no god but Allah.
I bear witness that Mohammed is the messenger of Allah.
Hasten to prayer. Hasten to success.
Allah is the greatest.
There is no god but Allah.

The *muezzin* (*above*) calls the faithful to prayer from the minaret. His role is important because the times of the call to prayer are determined by the sun and change daily. On Fridays, he chants special prayers and gives a sermon to the worshippers through a loudspeaker.

Before going into a mosque, shoes must be removed. Men and women have different entrances. After ritual washing, they enter separate areas of the mosque.

In some parts of Arabia, it is the custom for the women to pray privately in their own homes instead of attending the mosque.

In the Holy month of Ramadan, women frequently go to the mosque for the last prayer of the day, and also on the first day of Eid.

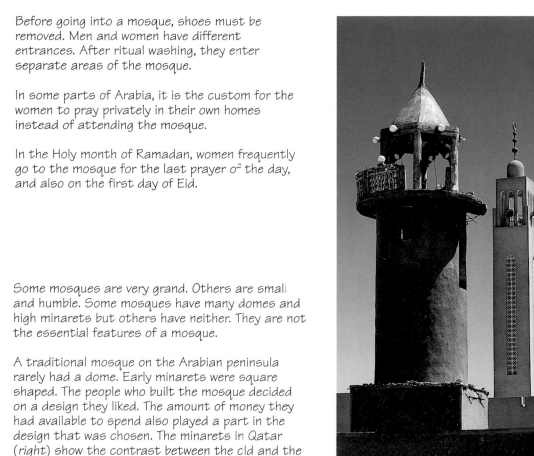

Some mosques are very grand. Others are small and humble. Some mosques have many domes and high minarets but others have neither. They are not the essential features of a mosque.

A traditional mosque on the Arabian peninsula rarely had a dome. Early minarets were square shaped. The people who built the mosque decided on a design they liked. The amount of money they had available to spend also played a part in the design that was chosen. The minarets in Qatar (*right*) show the contrast between the old and the new.

The design of a mosque

Important features of a mosque are

① courtyard   ② fountain   ③ qibla wall
④ minbar (steps for a preacher)   ⑤ mihrab
⑥ prayer hall   ⑦ minaret

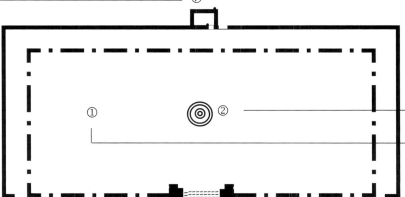

The minaret of the Prophet's Mosque in Madinah.

The courtyard and fountain of the Grand Mosque in Istanbul.

One of the niches in the qibla wall of the Grand Mosque of Oman.

The leader of the prayers speaks from a *minbar* or prayer pulpit. In some parts of Arabia the *minbar* is just a mat where the prayer leader stands, in others it is a carved staircase. The *minbar* of the Ibn Tulun Mosque in Cairo (right) is a good example of this.

The *mihrab* is the most important feature inside a mosque. It is an alcove in the wall of the mosque which faces towards Makkah. This wall is called the *qibla*. The qibla wall shows Muslims the direction in which they must pray. The mihrab is often elaborately decorated with all three elements of Islamic art — calligraphy, arabesques and geometric patterns.

On the outside of the mosque, the mihrab protrudes from the wall facing Makkah.

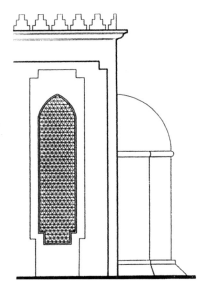

Every Bedu camp or tent had this mark scored on the surface of the ground indicating a communal prayer ground:

FACTOID!

The Grand Mosque at Makkah covers an area of 356,000 square metres. Although pilgrim visas are limited, more than two million pilgrims daily pack in to the Grand Mosque and its surrounding plazas during the pilgrimage. Escalators whisk 15,000 people an hour to the rooftop prayer areas.

For hundreds of years architects and craftsmen worked to beautify the design and decoration of mosques. Islamic art developed slowly as it spread out across the empire in the 7th century, but the essential features became clear and can be seen all over the world. These features are: geometric patterns, arabesques based on the form of plants, and calligraphy. Craftsmen worked for the glory of God, the Creator. They didn't seek fame and praise for themselves but remained anonymous. As the Prophet Mohammed condemned idolatry, pictures of people or animals were never used in sacred places. Craftsmen throughout the Islamic Empire decorated mosques using techniques that were traditional to the region where they lived. They copied artwork from the Roman and Persian empires, but added ideas of their own, gradually creating a unique style of Islamic art. In Arabia today, modern mosques are often decorated in designs that come from Syria, Iran or Egypt.

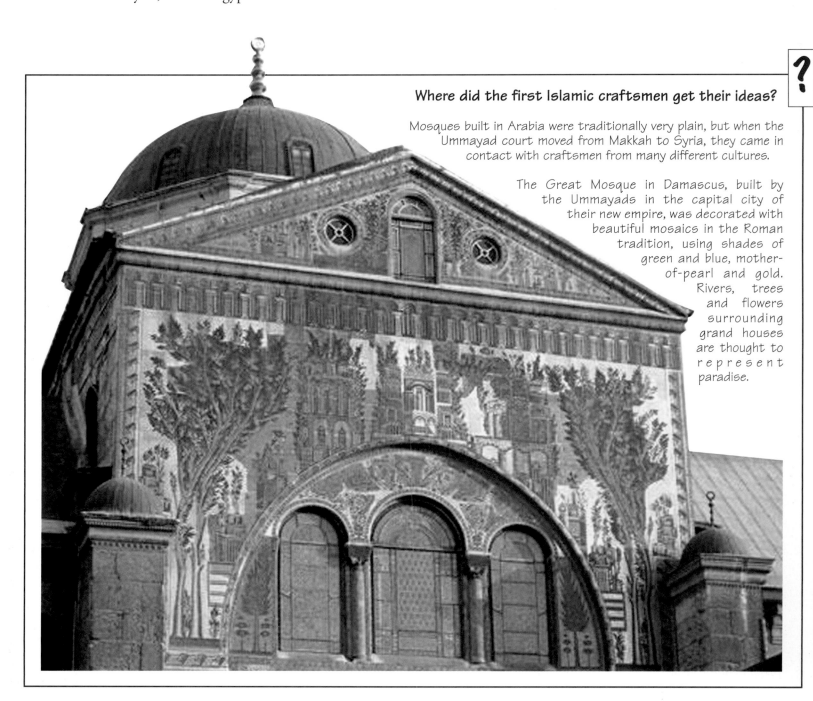

?

Where did the first Islamic craftsmen get their ideas?

Mosques built in Arabia were traditionally very plain, but when the Ummayad court moved from Makkah to Syria, they came in contact with craftsmen from many different cultures.

The Great Mosque in Damascus, built by the Ummayads in the capital city of their new empire, was decorated with beautiful mosaics in the Roman tradition, using shades of green and blue, mother-of-pearl and gold. Rivers, trees and flowers surrounding grand houses are thought to represent paradise.

Some examples of Islamic art:

Arabic calligraphy is at the heart of Islamic art. It is by far the most important feature. It is treasured because God's word, as written in the Koran, is sacred. Every mosque features calligraphy. Even if the writing is too high on the building to be read, just being there makes the mosque a special holy place, like the Grand Mosque in Oman (*left*).

The surfaces of mosques are often covered with tiles of brilliant colours and geometric shapes. A repeating pattern of shapes that fit together like pieces of a puzzle are called tessellations.

Arabesques are shapes taken from nature.

Flowers and leaves pass over and under each other, each weaving in and out to create patterns which are symmetrical and often enclosed by a geometric shape.

Below, an eight-pointed star has been decorated with inlaid wood of different colours and bone.

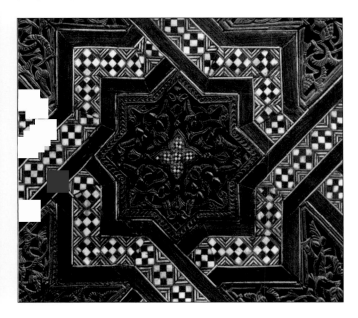

The Iranian mosque in Dubai is decorated with a combination of all the features of Islamic art.

There are many reminders throughout the Arabian peninsula that life was dangerous for people who lived in the towns and villages. They had to defend themselves against invaders from overseas and attacks from within the area. There were many disputes between neighbouring tribes over territory and water, so each community needed to be alert and ready for action. Large towns were often enclosed within a strong, high wall and could only be entered through the solid, wooden gateway during daylight hours. Forts guarded every town. Some were military buildings and others were castles, or fortified residences, where people lived. Forts provided a safe refuge and were built to withstand sieges or lengthy attacks. Watchtowers stood guard at strategic points so that early warning could be given of an enemy approaching. The design and layout of the defensive structures and the advanced building technology used in their construction can still be seen today. They are fine examples of the architectural heritage of the area.

A watchtower at Ras al Khaimah, United Arab Emirates, built facing the sea.

Defending the Fort

Forts were positioned as the first line of defence. Sometimes they were built on a craggy hill, facing the sea or standing guard over a flat plain. People a long way off could be watched as they approached the fort.

Forts had high towers and battlements. The battlements had narrow loopholes known as crenellations, which provided cover for people defending the fort.

Sometimes the stonework jutted out beyond the walls in beak-like projections. Arrows or guns could be aimed downwards when the enemy tried to storm the door or wall base.

Openings in the wall appeared very narrow from the front of the fort but they widened out behind the wall. The defender could stand and aim his arrows or firearms in all directions

Gates were weak spots in the defences. They were made of heavy wood and studded with metal spikes. A boiling brew made from the juice of dates, oil and honey could be poured through a recess above the door of the fort onto the heads of attackers below.

Port holes for cannons

Studded door

Larger openings lower down the walls were port holes for cannons which were mounted behind the walls. Cannons were introduced to the area by Portuguese invaders in the early 16th century and brought about changes in the design of forts. The best design for defending the fort with cannons was a square enclosure with two round towers on diagonally opposite corners. Walls were thickened to resist cannon fire and towers heightened to extend the range of guns.

Each region of Arabia developed its own style of defensive building, using the limited materials available.

Inside the forts, villagers needed food and water to last them for many weeks in case they were besieged. A well was dug in the central courtyard, or a falaj constructed underneath the fort. A storeroom was built for dates, which were their main source of food.

Larger forts had a special room for processing dates. The floor was ridged and covered with palm leaf matting. Heavy sacks of dates were piled on the matting (right). Their weight caused a sticky, sweet liquid to run from the dates, which was collected in jars set into the ground below.

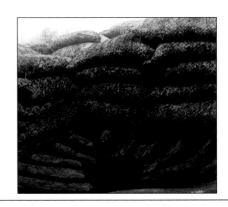

?

What kind of weapons would have been used in warfare?

1. Gun with gunpowder container. Gunpowder was made by grinding and mixing sulphur, charcoal and saltpetre.
2. Spear heads, which were dipped in vegetable poisons.
3. Arrows made from deer horn.
4. Swords and shields. Shields measured about 22 cm across. They were made from animal skins.

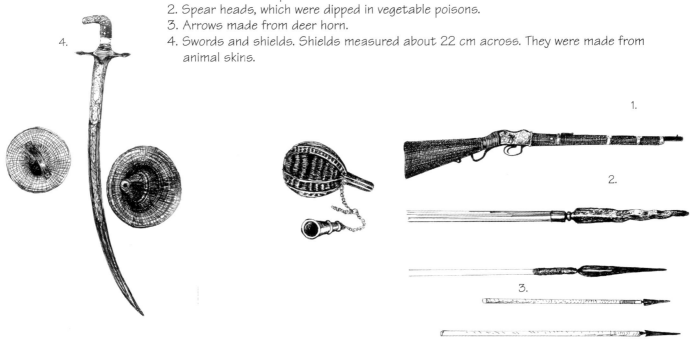

The *souq*, or market place, is traditionally an area of narrow shaded alleys lined with small single-storey shops. This style of *souq* has been in existence since pre-Islamic times, thousands of years ago, and is an important part of every town and village. One extensive and ancient *souq* at Qariat al-Fau, on the edge of the vast desert known as the Empty Quarter in Saudi Arabia, has recently been unearthed by archaeologists. It shows that trade has always been at the centre of life in Arabia, bringing wealth to its people. Today, *souqs* are still popular. They are a meeting place and bustle with noisy excitement as people visit the shops to buy goods. They are crammed full of goods, so bargaining and discounts are expected. Shops selling the same kind of goods are grouped together. Sometimes an entire *souq* will sell only one type of merchandise. The fish *souq*, the spice *souq* and the gold *souq* are just a few of the different *souqs* that can be found in all the large towns.

Doctors using traditional herbal medicines practised in the souqs. Although modern medicines are available today, many people still trust the old-fashioned remedies to cure them of common ailments. Jars, boxes and tins containing natural products are on sale.

Coffee shops provide meeting places where men smoke shisha pipes and discuss the events of the day. Shishas are ancient water pipes that have been used for centuries, long before the arrival of American cigarettes.

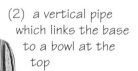

?

How does a shisha pipe work?

A shisha pipe consists of several different parts.

(1) a bowl where the tobacco is placed and lit by hot coals. Shisha tobacco is soaked in fruit shavings such as strawberry, apple or grapes. There is even a cola flavoured tobacco!

(2) a vertical pipe which links the base to a bowl at the top

(3) a hollow glass base, which is filled with water

(4) a long flexible hose, with a mouth-piece at the end.

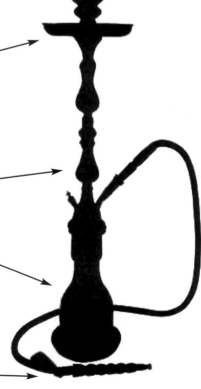

As the tobacco burns, the smoke is pulled down the pipe to the water-filled base by the smoker who is sucking on the hose. This changes the air pressure inside the pipe. The smoke is cooled by passing through water.

Gold souqs sparkle and dazzle in all the big towns. Gold is viewed as an investment, as well as being beautiful and luxurious to own. Jewellery made of gold can be traded in for more fashionable pieces or exchanged for cash. The price of gold in the souq is fixed to the world gold market and goes up and down daily. The purity of gold is measured in carats; 24 carat is the purest. None of the gold for sale in Arabia is less than 18 carat, which is much higher than 9 or 14 carat gold sold in many other parts of the world. Dubai has the largest import and export trade of gold in Arabia. Much of the gold goes to other Arab countries or India and Pakistan.

The gold souq in Riyadh (right).

Souqs are open from first light in the morning and closed again at nightfall, with a few hours of rest in the middle of the day for lunch and a nap. In the past, a massive door, set in an archway at the entrance of the souq, ensured the shops were secure during the night.

During the day, wooden shutters on the front of shops are thrown back and goods spill out onto the narrow alleyways outside.

Modern souqs have been built in some cities using traditional Islamic designs, like the Sharjah souq, United Arab Emirates (below).

In the past donkeys carried shopping home in panniers thrown across their backs. Today shopping goes home by car, but souqs have kept their appeal for friendliness and bustle. They are still popular for having the best deals.

PEARLS — WEALTH OF THE SEA

Although it is not known exactly when harvesting of pearls began in the waters of the Arabian Gulf, individual pearls have been found in archaeological digs dating from the late Stone Age. Pearls were often crushed and used for medicinal purposes. A local legend tells how they were thought to have magical qualities and even to hold the secret of eternal life which led King Galgamesh from Urak in Mesopatamia to seek 'this flower of immortality' from the bottom of the ocean. A 4,000-year-old pearl set in a gold earring, excavated in Bahrain, is the oldest example of a pearl being used as a gem. When Alexander the Great, leader of the Greek Empire, sent three ships to the Gulf more than 2,000 years ago, his admiral wrote of the highly prized pearls from Bahrain. He called them by their local name of *berberi*. Bahraini pearls are world famous for their unmatched lustre. There are unique conditions in this area where oysters containing pearls grow. Bahrain means **two seas** because fresh-water springs bubble to the surface and mix with the sea-water off its coasts. Also, hard substrata on the ocean floor is particularly suitable for their growth. These two factors are thought to produce the special qualities of Bahraini pearls. Pearl banks extended along the whole of the southern coastline of the Gulf, and major pearling centres grew up, providing work for all the region.

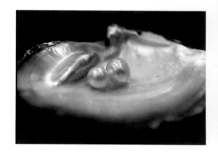

Pearling captains were known as *nakhudas*. The ruler of each local port appointed just one *nakhuda* to be in control of all the boats from that port. He would set the date and time for boats to leave for the pearl banks. Diving only took place in late spring and summer. All boats from the same port would set sail together and return approximately 120 days later. Sometimes boats stopped at one pearl bank for the entire season or moved to another depending on the decision of the *nakhuda*.

What equipment did a pearl diver need?

Water was prevented from entering the nose with clips made from turtle shell. The clips also helped to equalize pressure on the ears and air spaces within the head.

A cotton suit was put on to protect the skin against jellyfish.

Leather caps protected fingers from sharp shells.

A heavy stone or lead weight was attached to the diver by a line. He had to make sure he stayed in close touch with the line or the current might carry him away from the boat.

The diver had a basket hung round his neck. He placed oysters into the basket as quickly as possible. When he wanted to be hauled to the surface, he signalled to a puller on deck by tugging on the line.

How pearls are formed?

A piece of sand or grit gets inside the oyster shell which it finds irritating. Natural pearls also have parasites growing on their shells or maybe a small organism penetrates the shell and causes irritation.

The oyster begins to cover the grit or parasite with shell-like material, called nacre, from cells in its body. More and more layers are added until a pearl begins to develop.

The pearl takes on average 10 years to become mature. About twenty per cent of natural oyster shells contain a pearl.

Pearling boats (sambuks) were of various sizes. Some accommodated small crews of only a few men. Other very large boats had crews of 60 to 80 men. They rowed the boats to the pearling banks accompanied by a musician (nahham). As they worked they sang rhythmic chants, which are still remembered and sung at folk-lore events today.

The first set of divers would go down together. When they had collected the oysters they would return to the surface by the side of the boat until they had all finished diving. Each diver collected about eight to ten oysters every time he went down. They could only stay below the surface for one or two minutes.

On the boat, a second set of men waited. Their job was to pull baskets of oysters onto the deck. Then the divers came onto deck and exchanged jobs with the pullers who took their turn at diving. After diving repeatedly they were exhausted. It was a very hard life with few breaks during the day. A meal of fish and rice was cooked for the crew before everyone settled down on the crowded deck to sleep for the night. This was their routine every day during the diving season. Shore trips were made to pick up fresh water, dates, rice, coffee and tobacco for the crew.

FACTOID

Folk stories about how pearls are formed are passed down from generation to generation.

One popular story says that, when it rained, pearl oysters swam to the surface of the sea. There they opened their shells and a drop of rainwater fell into them, which turned into a pearl.

PEARLS — TRADERS AND TREATIES

During the 19th and early 20th century, pearls were the most valued export of the Arabian Gulf. Pearls were luxury items which rich people all over the world desired; they provided people in the Gulf with money to buy goods they needed from other countries. Merchants from India came to the area as pearls were traded through the international markets in Bombay and Baghdad. Owning and fitting out a pearling boat became big business. When the industry reached its height, about 4,200 boats were working on the pearl banks, employing around 30,000 men. However, in the 1930s, the industry came to an abrupt end. The Japanese flooded the market with cultured pearls and the pearl merchants of the Gulf could not compete with their prices. When the pearling industry collapsed, some people left the coastal towns to take up other work but many others became very poor. Those who had invested all their money in pearling and the boat building industry were financially ruined.

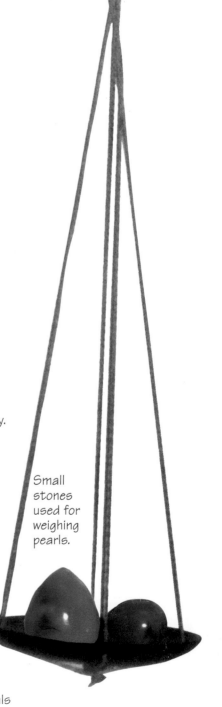

The red and white flag of Bahrain is symbolic of the white pearls and the red cloth in which they were wrapped.

? Which pearls were the most valuable?

Pearls were valued according to their quality. The shape, size, colour, lustre and imperfections were all important factors. A very large pearl was sold separately. Smaller pearls were sold by weight.

The sale of pearls was organised by the *nakhuda*. It was usual for him to sell the catch to a pearl merchant called a *tawwash* who in turn sold them on to a dealer from the international markets.

The pearls were balanced on one side of the scales. Small stones used as weights were put on the other side of the scales.

! FACTOID

Sieves were used to grade the pearls. There were five sieves with different sized holes. The biggeet holes were 4.6 mm wide, so only large pearls stayed behind in the sieve. The smallest holes were 2.8 mm wide.

The *nakhuda* took charge of the oyster shells brought up every day. After opening the shells, the oysters were returned to the pearling grounds that they were taken from. The crew benefited very little from all the hard work they put in. They borrowed money from the *nakhuda* to help with their living expenses and returned home little better off than when the season started. The following year they had to return once more to the pearling boats to pay off their debts.

A wooden box was used to contain the sorted pearls, which were wrapped in a red cloth called an *egmesh*. A notebook of the deals the *nakhuda* had made was also kept in the box.

Small stones used for weighing pearls.

Control of the pearling banks

The ports from which the boats sailed were controlled by the ruler of that area. However, there was no control over the pearling banks. They were open to any boat from Arab shores. Sometimes disputes broke out over who was allowed to take the pearls.

Regulations were drawn up to settle disputes at sea in a General Treaty of Peace which was signed by Bahrain and the rulers of the Sheikhdoms in 1820. It is an important document in the history of the region as it laid the foundations for the Trucial States, which were later to become the United Arab Emirates.

Bahrain is aclaimed as 'the King of Pearls'. The pearls fished in its waters were the finest in the world. At the height of the pearling industry, Bahrain had 917 boats.

Map from 1720, showing the pearl banks.

Who was Maria Theresa?

In the pearling deals, Maria Theresa dollars, known as thalers, were the accepted currency. Maria Theresa of Austria was the Empress of Austria who died in 1780. This is the date stamped on most of the thalers available today, although they would not have been minted in that year. The coins were first minted in 1751 and were so popular as the form of currency that, 150 years later, they were still being used. They were particularly popular for trading with countries in the East and Africa.

The reason they remained so popular was that people had faith in them. The silver content of the coins was always the same and it was difficult to clip the edge. Thalers were often melted down to make Bedouin jewellery. A popular style of necklace had thalers attached to it.

FACTOID

Forty-five million Maria Theresa thalers were minted during the first twelve years of the 20th century. The Royal Mint in London struck 6 million between 1945 and 1958

DHOWS

Row upon row of dhows line wharfs along the coast. The quays are piled high with goods of every kind. Crates of modern electrical equipment, satellite dishes, car tyres and foodstuffs are stacked side by side with old bicycles and cars. Everyone is busy as crews load cargo for the next trip. Trading by dhow has long been at the centre of life in the coastal towns. Today shipping companies, operating from huge container ports, have taken over much of the bulky, long distance business. However, local trade is still handled by dhows that transport goods up and down the Gulf and across the waters to Iran, India and Pakistan. Others follow the coastline to the southern shores of Arabia before crossing to the east coast of Africa. The word *dhow*, commonly used to describe all trading boats, is an Indian word. In Arabic, the boats are known by their individual names. *Boom, sambuk* and *jalibut* are some of the types most often used today. The days of sail are long past and dhows are now fitted with modern diesel engines.

When dhows arrive at a port they must visit the Customs Office where the cargo is inspected and taxes paid on the goods. Police are on the look out for smuggling of drugs or illegal immigrants.

In the past bidding took place for the goods after they were unloaded. It was an anxious time for the crew as they waited to find out how much money had been made on the journey. Nowadays, goods are ordered and bought before their arrival at the port.

Until the 1970s, the Arabian Gulf had few natural harbours. Ships had to moor offshore and goods were transferred into smaller craft to take them to land. *Shamal* winds and high seas often proved too hazardous for shipping and they were wrecked. All the ports now have deep-water berthage to allow dhows to offload in the centre of towns. Many small ports and fishing harbours have been constructed along the coast.

Cargo is piled high on the quayside. At the end of May the monsoon winds control movement of the ships. Even though engines have replaced sails to power the dhows, heavy swells and high waves make journeys difficult. Dhows stay in port for the next four months or trade within the Gulf or Red Sea, which are not affected by the monsoon.

Boards along the wharfage advertise where the dhows are going. Anyone wanting to send their goods to that destination can buy space on the dhow.

Booms can carry loads of 200-500 tonnes and are the principal ocean-going cargo and passenger vessels.

Sambuks carrying loads of 60-80 tonnes, and the smaller shu'i, are used for general cargo and passenger work.

Life aboard the dhow lacks modern comforts

The *nakhuda*, the master of the vessel, has a cabin on deck. He oversees the work of the crew as they load and unload the cargo and maintain the dhow in good condition. The *nakhuda* may buy and sell cargo for the owner. He may also be a part-owner of the vessel. The principal owner usually lives ashore and does not travel with the dhow.

Toilets, known as *zoolies*, are hung over the back of the boat.

There is no room below deck for crew accommodation. The hull is filled with cargo. The crew sleep where they can on deck among the cargo being carried. Boats have about 18-20 crew. Although living quarters lack modern comforts, the dhows are equipped with the latest navigation systems using satellites to give them their position at sea.

! A 13th century painted manuscript, Al-Hariri's 'Maqamat' from Baghdad, shows the way of life in Arabia in great detail (*above*). Although not completely accurate in all its details, it is possible to see how a trading dhow 800 years ago was very similar to ones operating in Arabia today. Merchants aboard the ship are peering from the open windows. From their headdresses it can be seen that they came from all parts of the world.

FACTOID

Dhows built for speed! Unlike the big, heavy trading dhows, racing dhows are built for speed, with shallow hulls. Huge fleets of more than 100 boats can be seen regularly gliding like swans across the waters of the Gulf. Prizes for the winners of each race are over 100,000 dirhams.

Building and repairing of dhows is an expensive business. Small dhows are still built along the coast but not many large dhows. A new material, fibreglass, is replacing wood as it is cheap and longlasting.

FISHING

For thousands of years, fish and dates were the main diet of people on the long coastline of the Arabian peninsula. Fish were of an excellent quality and so plentiful that travellers visiting Arabia were amazed at the catches they saw and described them in their journals. Traditional fishing methods had little effect on the quantity of fish in the ocean. Boats had to be rowed or sailed to the fishing grounds, and the nets and traps made from natural materials were biodegradable. If they were lost, they would quickly disintegrate. Fishermen knew the times of the year when fish bred and allowed young fish to mature to a large size before catching them. It seemed that fish would always be there as a renewable resource. However, the number of fishing boats has increased enormously over the last twenty years. Equipped with motorised engines and modern equipment over-fishing is a growing problem. Small catches of fish each night bothers fishermen. Small fish for sale in the market bothers buyers who remember when large specimens were always available. Fish from the sea are a beautiful inheritance but like all other creatures their needs must be respected if they are to remain plentiful in the future.

A man fishing with a cast net

Below: A fishing boat laying gill nets.

Right: Tiny fish such as anchovies and sardines are laid out to dry on the beach. They are made into fertilizer or feed for stock. Many tons are exported.

What are the different ways that fish are caught?

Cast nets

Cast nets (*opposite*) are circular and weighted at the edge. The net is thrown onto the water, and quickly gathered in by one person. Small fish such as sardines are caught using these nets, which may be used for food or baiting hooks.

Fish traps

Fishermen can be seen raking up seaweed on the mud flats at low tide. This is crushed and used inside the traps as bait. In the past these circular traps, laid on the seabed, were made from palm fronds which were biodegradable.

Today traps are made of wire and are frequently lost on the seabed. Many fish trapped in them die needlessly. If a piece of biodegradable rope was used tc hold the trap door closed, this would eventually disintegrate allowing fish in lost traps to escape.

Al Hadrah traps

On many shores of the Arabian Gulf large quantities of fish are caught in hadrah traps. Traditionally they were made from palm frond branches bound together with string, but these materials have now been replaced with wire netting. They are constructed in shallow waters adjacent to the beach. At the water's edge, the barriers lead into circular, trianglar or pentagonal shaped traps.

At high tide fish swim in to feed. As the tide falls, or when fish come up against the long walls of the traps, they try to make their way back to deep water. Swimming along the barriers they are led into traps at the end. There they stay until low tide when fishermen walk across the sand to the traps, and spear or net the fish. There are several other methods used to catch fish by placing barriers across shallow waters.

Seine nets

In the past imported cotton was used to make Seine nets. Pieces of palm trunk were attached to the top of the net as floats. The nets could be 100 metres long but were usually much shorter. They were laid parallel to the shore. Fishermen on the beach gradually pulled the net in. This method of fishing is used today with nets made from modern materials. Two speed-boats lay the nets, and four wheel-drive vehicles pull them up the beach.

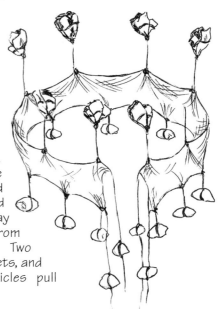

Gill nets

As night falls, fishing boats set sail to lay their nets. Gill nets (*far left*), used for catching

larger fish are shot out over the side of the boat. Made of nylon nowadays, with pieces of polystyrene or rubber floats, these nets can be 100 metres long and 10 metres deep. The next morning the fishermen collect the catch.

Dugongs, dolphins and turtles are among the many creatures that have to face the dangers of gill nets every night. Many are trapped needlessly along with fish destined for the souq.

Hook, line and sinker

Large fish are also caught by hook and line. Tuna, barracuda and mackerel are caught on lines baited with sardines. As many as twenty large fish can be caught by a skilled fisherman in a few hours by this method. Long lines with twenty or more hooks are used to catch sharks and groupers.

THE FISH SOUQ

Every morning hundreds of harbours along the long coastline of Arabia bustle with activity as the day's fishing catch is landed. After oil, fishing is the most commercially productive activity in the region. People gather round, curious to see what is on offer. Heaped into baskets, laid out in neat rows, piled in high mounds every seller tries to attract customers with the quality and freshness of his fish. Agents wait nearby, anxious to get a supply of the highly valued species such as *safee*, lobsters and shrimp at a good price. Open trucks, loaded with ice-filled cool boxes stand ready to transport fish to inland towns. At the end of the *souq* a group of men flash their knives swiftly. Fish livers and eggs are sold, but heads and bones are swept into a pile at their feet. The customer departs with his fish in a plastic bag, cleaned for only a few small coins. In a few hours, business is completed for the day. The floor is hosed down with water and the market is silent until tomorrow.

Large deep sea fish for sale include mackerel, tuna, jacks and trevallys with smooth silvery skin.

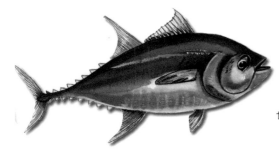

Tuna can be over two metres long and weigh from 10 to 30 kilos. These large fish are commercially important as they are suitable for canning.

Spanish mackerel or kingfish, one of the largest fish for sale in the souq, is often bought by the slice. It is good value for money.

Barracuda are thin, elongated fish with sharp teeth. They range from 50 centimetres to two metres long.

A wide variety of fish are on sale in the souq.

Baby shark can be eaten fresh if they are small, but more often they are dried and salted.

Rabbit fish, locally called safee, are a good buy. The body of a rabbit fish has very small scales and smooth skin, heavily covered with silvery-white spots.

FACTOID

GET YOUR FISH CLEANED FOR JUST $1

In one corner of the fish souq, a big army of men with sharp knives clean and gut the fish for you in seconds.

Fish eyes are considered very tasty and are removed to be sold separately.

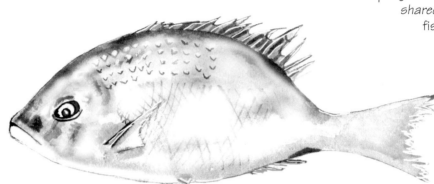

Spangled emperors, locally called sharee, are highly prized food fish. A Spangled emperor can be 85 cm long.

Large hamour is a general name for several species of grouper. They are one of the most popular fish and attract many purchasers. Large hamour can grow to almost two metres but they are often over-fished resulting in very small ones being offered for sale.

Cuttlefish and squid are white or mottled creatures with eight arms. Their flat, tapering, white cuttlebone is given to caged birds to improve their beaks.

Red snapper are frequently for sale but their colour is more pink than red. There are many species of popular, cheap snapper in the market.

Lobsters and shrimp are the most expensive items on sale. They are valuable exports and sent to many countries in the world. During their breeding season in the spring, the fishing season for shrimp is closed and they are not available in the souqs.

WATER — SOURCE OF LIFE

Water is the most important need for life. In a desert region where rainfall is scarce people can only settle in places where they can obtain a regular supply. When rain falls it enters underground storage systems called aquifers. Thousands of years ago, in a time when heavy rain fell on the Arabian peninsula, a vast underground reservoir of water as large as an ocean was formed that stretched right across Arabia. Oases sprang up in places where it came near to the surface. Water is distributed from aquifers by wells and *falaj* irrigation channels. Advanced engineering technology used in constructing the *falaj* system goes back thousands of years. This method of distributing water was also used in Persia so it may have been introduced to Arabia from across the seas. Each source of water was carefully guarded. The *falaj* is essential to community life in the village.

How was time measured before there were clocks?

?

In many towns and villages there is a sun clock which measures the time that is due to each owner. A post of wood or metal, or vertical stone stuck into the ground creates a sun clock. The sun and the shade act as hands on the clock. A line of small stones set in the ground marks the beginning and end of each person's share during daylight. When the shadow falls on a new stone, the owner of that share knows the time has arrived for irrigating his land.

The job of monitoring the water in the *falaj* to make sure that each owner gets his correct share goes on day and night. One villager is in charge of this work, but he appoints deputies to help him with the task. At night the position of the stars is used to mark the beginning and end of a person's share of water.

A weaving done by village women shows chores taking place along the *falaj*.

How did a typical falaj work?

One type of falaj consists of a long tunnel dug towards underground springs at the foot of the mountains. It brings the water up above the ground near the village, where it is distributed in open channels. The tunnel may be several kilometres long. There are vertical shafts into the tunnel every 50 metres or so which are normally closed at the top. They were used to take the gravel and stone out long ago when the tunnel was built and are used today to maintain the tunnel in good condition and clean out silt.

Water flowing underground. A 'mother well' is dug to this level.

Tunnel carries water to the village

Water distributed to the village

Vertical shafts used to maintain the tunnel

Another type of falaj consists of an open channel which brings water straight from a spring in the mountain. When the spring is a long way from land suitable for farming, the water flows into a stone tank which has a plug at the bottom. When it is full the plug is taken out and the water is then emptied into a larger channel and flows much faster. Without this the water would dry up in the heat of the sun before it ever reached the village.

Left: a falaj with an open channel.

!

FACTOID

A falaj may vary from a small trickle to a large flow depending on whether there has been a recent rainfall or there are drought conditions. A typical falaj might have a flow of 40 litres per second, enough to provide the needs of a village of about 1,000 people.

The distribution of water is very carefully controlled in the village. The rights of everyone who owns a share of the water are recorded in falaj books. More than 200 people in each village may be involved in sharing water.

Every person owning a share in the falaj has a set amount of time for irrigating his land. The small channels to the fields and date gardens are blocked with stones or pieces of wood when irrigation is not taking place.

Water coming into the village is used in order of priority (below). Clean water for drinking must not be polluted by other activities taking place along the falaj but nowadays drinking water is piped or delivered to houses by tanker.

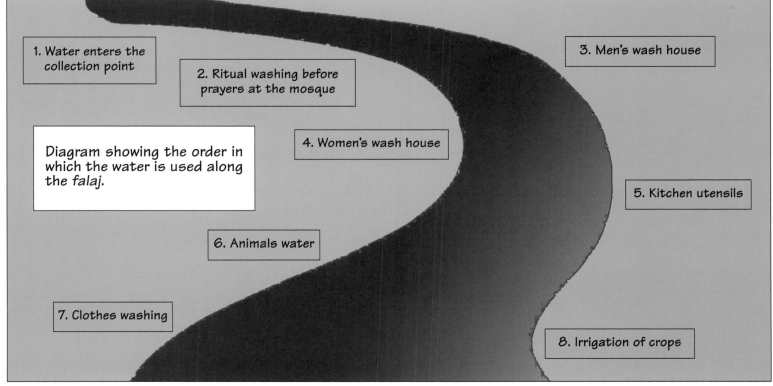

1. Water enters the collection point

3. Men's wash house

2. Ritual washing before prayers at the mosque

4. Women's wash house

Diagram showing the order in which the water is used along the falaj.

5. Kitchen utensils

6. Animals water

7. Clothes washing

8. Irrigation of crops

THE DATE PALM

Cultivating the date palm has always been by far the most important form of agriculture on the Arabian peninsula. Archaeologists have found evidence that dates were cultivated over 7,000 years ago. In ancient times Muslim travellers took date palm seedlings with them on their journeys. The fruit is so nutritious that it is possible to survive on dates and milk alone. Long desert journeys were only possible because a supply of dates could be taken along to eat when nothing else was available. The pearling ships had fresh dates delivered to them throughout the season, and sailors setting off on long voyages took supplies of dates with them. The date palm is a very special tree, and holds a very special place in the hearts and minds of the people of the Arabian peninsula. Of the 90 million date palms in the world, 64 million grow in Arab countries.

Can trees be male or female?

Yes, palm trees are male or female. Only the female trees bear fruit, so more of them are planted than the male tree. The best trees can produce 50 to 100 kilos of dates every year.

The male palms produce a comb of pollen ladened flowers. The pollen has to be taken to the female palms so that fertilisation can take place. It is usually the work of insects, such as bees, to pollinate flowers, but they cannot be relied upon to do this important job in the date gardens. The farmer extracts some branches from the male comb and ties them among the female sprays. The female tree can produce dates when it is around 8 years old.

Can 100,000 new palm trees be grown from just one plant? Modern technology shows how it can be done.

A palm tree is usually grown from a shoot that comes up at the foot of the tree.

A method of growing trees called Plant Tissue Culture has been developed. This method makes sure that many more of the best types of palm tree can be grown than would happen naturally.

The shoot tip is removed from the tree that is to be reproduced. This is cut into small pieces, only the size of a human tooth. Each piece is put into a special jelly-like growth medium full of nutrients in a test-tube.

The test-tubes are kept in a warm, sterile place with the nutrients changed regularly. Between six months to a year later, the piece of tissue develops many buds. Each of these buds can develop a shoot which grows into a new tree. The new tree has exactly the same good qualities as the mother tree. An amazing number of new trees can be developed from one shoot tip.

Owning date palms is very important to the people of Arabia. But in rural areas people have moved away to the towns to work, often leaving date gardens untended, so the trees eventually die.

Date palms are used to make cities green and attractive. When the United Arab Emirates was founded in 1972 it had 2,000,000 palm trees. In the year 2001 there were 40,000,000 trees and the number continues to grow.

!

FACTOID

Saudi Arabia has over 250 varieties of dates.

What must the date farmer do to make his trees grow?

A palm frond

A rib runs down the centre of the frond.

Leaves grow on each side of the rib.

In date gardens old branches are removed each year, forcing new branches to sprout higher.

The leaf is shaped like a feather, *reeshah* in Arabic. The word *areesh* comes from it and is used to describe palm frond houses.

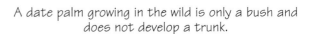

Steps are formed from the stumps of the cut off branches which are convenient for men to climb up to harvest the ripe dates.

A date palm growing in the wild is only a bush and does not develop a trunk.

When the dates are ready for harvesting in July and August, the farmer climbs the tree by looping a long rope made from palm tree fibres around the trunk and gradually works his way to the top. His back is supported so he has both hands free to pick the dates. He puts them in his basket, which is woven from leaves of the tree. Dates are picked before they are fully ripe (*left*) because they would shrivel up in the heat if left on the tree to ripen.

Not all the date crop is eaten when freshly picked. Sacks, made from leaves of the date palm tree, are packed with dates that have been boiled. Dates can last for months.

Some of the many varieties of dates grown in Saudi Arabia

Bullocks (*right*) were used to pull up water from wells to irrigate the date palms. A man would lead the bullock up a slope from the head of the well to lift water in a leather bag, which was then emptied into a stone tank. Once full, the plug was pulled out and the water flowed into channels to water the land. Date palms can grow even if watered with brackish and salty water, which would kill most other plants. Nowadays these wells have mechanical pumps instead of using animals to raise water to the surface.

USES OF THE DATE PALM

Settlements grew up in places where there was water for palm trees, either from the *falaj* system or from wells. In hot summer months, many people from the coast and the desert would move to the cooler areas of the date gardens to join in the important work of harvesting dates. Everything was packed up for the move. Chickens, kitchen utensils, bedding and the women of the tribe were loaded onto camels. Goats were herded along behind. As well as providing nourishment, the date palm was used to build houses and animal enclosures. A variety of everyday items were made from the leaves. Houses made from palm fronds were cool in the summer. In winter they could be made warmer by adding extra leaves or lining the walls with palm frond matting.

Some palm frond houses had a windtower (*above*) added to increase the circulation of air through the rooms. Wind-towers were made out of poles and sacking. When the winter weather made the windtower unnecessary, it was taken down and stored until needed again.

The date palm leaf has a hard rib in the centre. It narrows towards the top. The walls of palm frond houses are made of stripped palm leaf stems which are tied together top-to-tail to make the panels even.

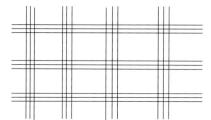

A trellis-like pattern could also be cut into the walls where more air was needed to make the house cool.

Mats of all kinds were used on the floor. Some were for sitting on and some were for placing trays of food on.

Covers for food were important items to keep out the flies and dust.

Household items are usually woven by women, as shown *below*.

Some fishermen used a shashah – a boat made entirely from palm fronds. The space between the hull and deck was filled with palm fronds and the keel was stuffed with palm bark to give it more bouyancy. One or two people could stay afloat on it as they rowed a little way out from the shore to lay their nets.

Fish traps were also made from palm fronds. The ribs were sliced in half down the centre and soaked in water for two days. They were then cut into suitable lengths for weaving. A slightly curved triangular shape was made to block the exit of the trap. This could be removed when it was time to extract the catch of fish.

To weave a leaf it must be cut off the hard rib at the centre of the frond. Each leaf is peeled in half lengthways and the edges removed. Finally it is shredded into several strands before being dyed and woven into long braids. The braids are then sewn together.

Chickens were sometimes kept in palm frond cages whilst waiting for the pot or being carried around. The cages were made from two ribs of the fronds.

Handmade baskets, mats and food covers on display in the souq.

Although many items have been replaced with modern materials, such as plastic or wire, shops still sell palm frond wares. They are popular buys with tourists.

A weaver putting the handles on a palm frond basket.

THE BEDOUIN

The people of the desert are the Bedouin. They are called the Bedu in Arabia. In the past they roamed freely over the Arabian peninsula, recognising no borders, in search of grazing for their camels. They lived under some of the most difficult and harsh conditions that man had to face anywhere in the world. The strength of character that developed from living with such hardships was greatly admired. Important *sheikhs* of the region are proud to acknowledge their links with the Bedu and the desert way of life. The Bedu know that they can depend on their families and tribe to help them in times of need. They are known for their great generosity and hospitality towards anyone they meet. The Bedu believe the camel is a special gift to them from God. They write poetry about it. They drink its milk, eat its meat and trade it to buy other goods they need. But times are changing. The areas where they can roam now are more limited. Also the Bedu have accepted that modern facilities, such as hospitals and schools, are good for their communities. They want to share in the wealth that oil has brought to the region.

Some Bedu were born under the welcome shade of a *ghaf* tree. Leaves and seed pods from *ghaf* trees were a valuable source of food for their livestock.

When the Bedu went in search of fresh vegetation for their camels, they could only take with them essentials which could be easily carried.

The Bedu still keep herds of goats, sheep and camels but camels are the animals closest to their hearts. Their ability to survive in the desert enabled people to travel long distances in an age when there was no other form of transport. In return, the Bedu looked after the camels by seeking good grazing areas, water holes (*above*) and taking care of their general health and well-being.

Choosing a leader

The nobles of the Bedu are called sheikhs. A sheikh governs all his family and tribe. When the sheikh becomes too weak, or dies, the leading chiefs of the tribe choose a successor. The whole tribe takes the name of his family and he becomes the authority for that tribe. The sheikh is obliged to regard his people as allies, rather than subjects as a king would do. He seeks their support, and has to keep working hard to justify his role as leader.

Raids on different tribes happened frequently in the past. Often the dispute was about the ownership of camels or blood feuds between tribes that wanted revenge for past quarrels.

An important part of Arabic culture is preserved in the lifestyle of the desert dwellers. When they gather together, the older people retell stories from their history to the new generations. Poetry is memorised and recited and songs are sung.

Bedu men have long been well-armed with rifles, ammunition, a *khanjar*, or dagger. Strength and courage were greatly admired by both men and women. A brave warrior in raids was well-thought-of amongst his tribe.

Today it is difficult to be a nomad but their traditions are a valuable part of the heritage of the Arabian peninsula.

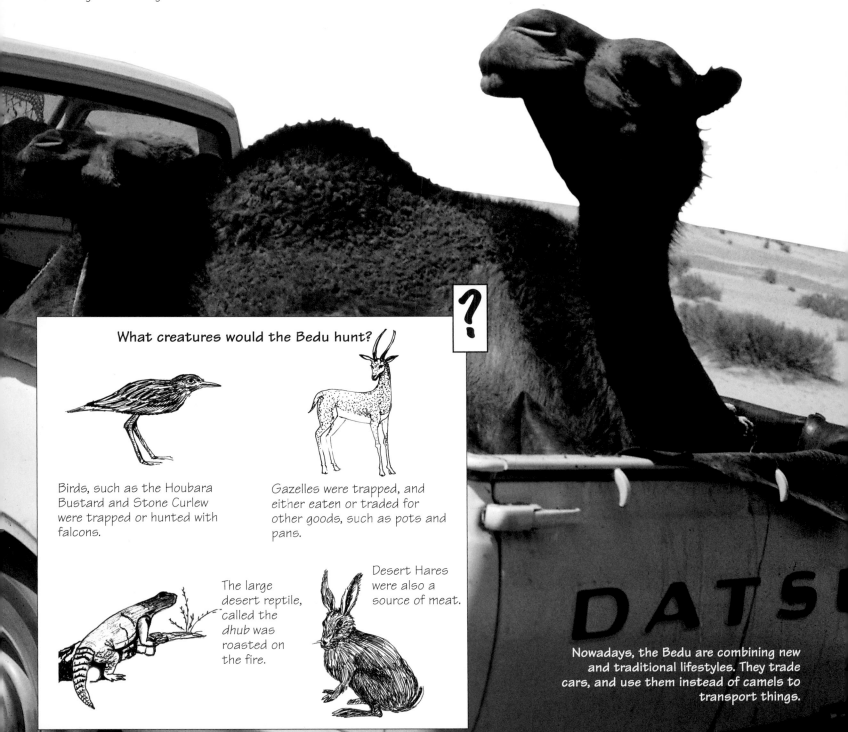

What creatures would the Bedu hunt?

Birds, such as the Houbara Bustard and Stone Curlew were trapped or hunted with falcons.

Gazelles were trapped, and either eaten or traded for other goods, such as pots and pans.

The large desert reptile, called the dhub was roasted on the fire.

Desert Hares were also a source of meat.

Nowadays, the Bedu are combining new and traditional lifestyles. They trade cars, and use them instead of camels to transport things.

THE BEDOUIN — LIFE IN A TENT

The traditional Bedu tent was made of dark brown or black strips of material. Goat hair was used to make the cloth, but sometimes sheep's wool was mixed with it. The size of the tent depended on the wealth of its owner. A *sheikh* may have had a tent 15 metres or more long, supported by four poles. A poor man would only have a tent about 5 metres long with two poles to hold it up. The tent was divided by two or three curtains into rooms. Pitching the tent was always carried out by the women of the tribe with the help of servants. When the tent was pitched the women placed their treasures, kitchen utensils and stores in the centre part of the tent. In the men's portion of the tent a carpet was rolled out, and coffee jugs set out. Guests were always welcome and made comfortable.

Water bottles were made from goats' skins.

A tent neighbour
Anyone who pitched their tent close to a fellow Bedu's tent became his tent neighbour and enjoyed many privileges. A member of another tribe, even if it was an unfriendly one, could ask if he could camp close by and join in the migration when the tribe moved. The tent neighbour was then treated like a guest, or a 'dear one'. Very complicated rules applied to the way he was treated but he was always given protection.

A litter
Women of some Bedu tribes travelled in a covered-in saddle, known as a litter. They perched on the camel's back inside the litter, surrounded by their belongings. The litter was covered with black cloth so that they were hidden from view.

!

FACTOID

The salt bond

For three nights after a guest had eaten food at a Bedu camp, he was protected from any harm from the tribe. This was called 'the salt bond'.

While the food was still in his stomach, he was safe.

The coffee ritual

Arabian coffee originates from Mocha in Yemen where it is grown on terraces built into the steep hillsides. All over Arabia making and serving coffee is a sign that a guest is welcome and honoured by his host. It is served in small cups without handles. The host holds the coffee pot in his left hand and, with three or four cups in his right hand, he walks around his guests filling their cups with coffee. The guest can have the cup refilled as many times as he likes. When the guest has had enough coffee he shakes the empty cup with little movements of his wrist, and the cup is removed by the host.

Guests at the tent

A stranger has to approach the tent from the front. It is considered very bad manners to arrive at the back. He must halt and make his camel kneel some way off. This shows he wants food or to stay for the night. The women also have time to put on their masks, called burqas, or veils. Every Bedu, rich or poor, must entertain and feed a stranger who asks for a night's lodging.

Tent dogs

Every tent had its own watchdogs. They were fierce creatures that were expected to guard the camels and sheep against wolves or strangers. They slept outside the tent and were thought to be unclean. Saluki dogs, however, were allowed inside the tents because they were useful on hunting trips. A saluki is a very fast dog reaching speeds of 60 km an hour. It can match the speed of a gazelle.

There is evidence from archaeological digs that the skills of spinning and weaving have been carried on in Arabia for more than 5,000 years. Many items necessary for everyday life were woven and skills were passed down from one generation to the next. Different methods of weaving the wool developed, depending on whether the people led a settled life or were nomadic and had to carry their looms with them. In towns and villages, men were the weavers. They used looms which were built over a pit. Shepherds and Bedu women also wove when they had the time or needed some woven item. Many different types of cloth are imported into Arabia today making it easier to buy rather than to make things but some traditional crafts are still practised.

Different methods developed for spinning (*right*). Both shepherds and Bedu women practised the skill of spinning using a spindle.

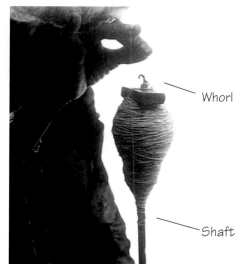

Whorl

Shaft

Wool from sheep and hair from goats (*above*) and camels is spun onto spindles in preparation for weaving. Camels do not have much wool on them. The very fine scales on the outer layer of sheep's wool enables it to be spun more easily than goat hair which produces prickly, strong yarn. Cotton was widely cultivated and also imported from India for weaving, as was silk. Goat hair is still used to make tents.

Bedu women spin with the whorl at the top of the shaft, whereas shepherds spin with the whorl at the bottom.

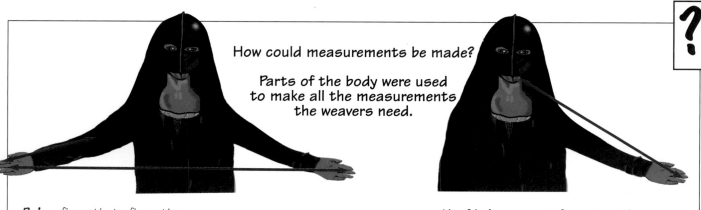

?

How could measurements be made?

Parts of the body were used to make all the measurements the weavers need.

Ba'a – fingertip to fingertip
Dhra' – elbow to fingertips (to measure the length of the warp).

Nusf ba'a – nose to fingertip with one arm outstretched.

Fiter – thumb to forefinger outstretched

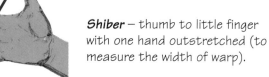

Shiber – thumb to little finger with one hand outstretched (to measure the width of warp).

Traditional designs (*left*) were woven into the cloth. Red was made from roots of the madder plant.

A loom is a simple device for keeping the warp threads under tension. The ground loom (*right*) was used by the Bedu. Parts of this loom were made from wood found locally in the desert.

Weaving involves two sets of threads called the warp and the weft that interlace with each other.

Warp and Weft

Warp are the threads that run the length of the loom and must be kept under tension.

Weft are the threads woven across the width of the loom.

For weaving to take place the warp threads must be separated into two layers so that the weft can be passed between them.

The space between the two layers is called the shed. A shed stick is used to keep the threads separated (*see below*).

The upper and lower warp threads have to change position after the weft threads have passed between them. String loops called heddles are attached to the lower warp threads so all the lower threads can be moved into the top position.

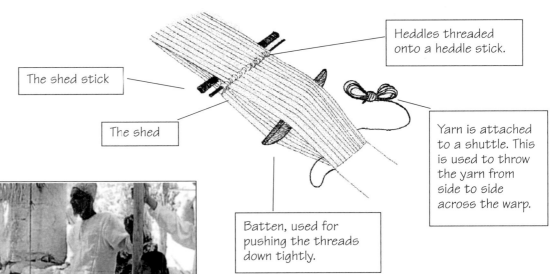

Heddles threaded onto a heddle stick.

The shed stick

The shed

Yarn is attached to a shuttle. This is used to throw the yarn from side to side across the warp.

Batten, used for pushing the threads down tightly.

The great camel caravans which once travelled throughout the Arabian peninsula used woven trappings on the camels.

Although the camel is not used for transport nowadays, camel racing is a popular sport and trappings (*below*) for the riding camel are still woven.

Pit looms (*above*) were used by settled villagers who had no need to move.

The weaver sits on the edge of a pit with his feet at the bottom, leaving his hands free to throw the shuttle. His feet operate the pedals which raise and lower alternate warp threads making a shed through which the shuttle is thrown.

The advantage of the pit loom is that longer pieces of material can be woven.

TRADITIONAL CRAFTS: JEWELLERY AND METALWORK

In the past, each town had craftsmen making jewellery and luxurious household items, as well as basic metal utensils for the home. The craft of metalworking is a fine skill and the craftsmen of some cities became famous for the quality of the work that was produced there. Jewellery has always been a very important part of a woman's possessions. When a woman marries, part of her dowry is paid in jewellery. It is hers to keep or to sell as she wishes. It is also the custom for her husband to give her beautiful pieces in celebration of their marriage and later on, when she becomes a mother, she is rewarded with more precious jewellery.

Traditionally, the pieces that were made from silver were melted down on her death as a new bride would want to have jewellery made specially for her. Old pieces are therefore rare and very expensive, so much of the silver on sale in souqs today is newly made.

The curved dagger, the *khanjar*, is worn by men in all parts of Arabia. Once the main weapon of war, today they are worn for their attractive appearance as an item of adornment. The design differs from one country to another. The *khanjars* made in Oman are known for their high level of workmanship and the good quality of silver used. Khanjars are worn on webbing or leather belts, to which they are attached by silver rings.

A curved dagger is called a *jambia* in Yemen. The sheath of the *jambia* is covered with green dyed leather webbing rather than silver.

?

Why was jewellery important to the Bedouin women?

In a society that was constantly on the move, a woman's money was solely in what she could carry, unlike townsfolk who also had wealth in land. It was common for women to own large amounts of silver jewellery which showed her importance in the tribe.

All parts of her body were decorated with heavy silver items, as the weight of the piece was the most important factor in deciding how much it was worth.

Precious possessions were often kept in large wooden chests which were decorated with thin brass plates, cut into different designs. Brass tacks with rounded heads were often arranged in patterns over the surface of the chest. A large lock made sure the contents were kept safely inside.

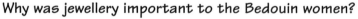

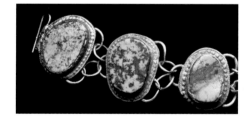

Sometimes coral, amber, glass or semi-precious stones were added to the silver. Some items were also worn to protect the wearer against evil.

Coffee Pots

The preparation and serving of coffee is a favourite pastime in Arabia. It is always produced for guests and made many times a day. The shape of the coffee pot varies from region to region and it is possible to tell which part of Arabia a pot comes from, depending on its shape and design.

The hourglass shape is very common with a wide, curved spout and a lid which comes to tall point.

Some are simple, and made of brass. Others are ornate, made of copper and silver. Patterns are made by hammering a design onto the metal.

Household items

Incense is used every day to perfume a house, or clothes so an incense burner is an important item in the household. Incense burners are beautifully embossed and engraved. Very elaborate ones have a hinged lid. Some, like the one on the right, are made of wood, studded with brass and inlaid with glass.

Items used around the house are often made of silver. Traditional silver items are sold in antique shops in the souqs. Kohl, used as eyeliner, was kept in small silver pots (*left*). A stick attached to the top was used to apply the khol around the eyes.

Small sets of tweezers, toothpicks and even a little spoon for cleaning out wax from ears were made from silver too.

FALCONRY

Falcons are birds of prey, adapted by nature to hunt live creatures. Falconry is the art of hunting with them. The birds are trained by the falconer and a partnership is formed between them. The two species traditionally used for hunting are the Peregrine and Saker falcons. The Peregrine falcon is the fastest bird in the world, plunging at 300 kilometres per hour. She uses her talons to punch her prey, knocking it to the ground. The falcon is admired for her courage and endurance. Her picture is often used as a symbol for these qualities. Currency, stamps, petrol stations and aeroplanes in Arabia all have pictures of the falcon on them. The creatures that are hunted are called the quarry. The traditional quarry is the Houbara Bustard and Stone Curlew. In some areas, Desert Hares are also hunted. Training falcons and hunting with them is looked upon as a noble art in Arabia and is admired and respected.

The falconer 'mans' the falcon, which means 'makes her tame.' He keeps the falcon with him at all times while she is being tamed. Sheikhs traditionally employ falconers to train their birds for them. The falconer has special equipment used for training and handling his bird, which is known as 'the furniture'. When out hunting he carries a hawking bag, a *mikhla*, which is shaped like a square sack.

jesses, *subuq*, are fitted to each of the bird's ankles.

The falcon has a hood, *burqa*, placed over her head when she is not hunting. This keeps her calm and quiet.

The perch, *wakir*, has a padded surface on which the falcon rests. Some of them have a spike on the end which is pushed into the sand. A modern material for the falcon to rest on comfortably is astroturf.

FACTOID

A fortnight at most is all that a good falconer needs to train a young bird. If it is already two to three years old, it will take longer; up to three weeks will be needed for it to learn to hunt.

Below, the lure, tilwah, which plays an important part in training a falcon. It is a bundle of feathers which the falconer swings round his head. The falcon is encouraged to land on it with a reward of a piece of meat. Eventually the falcon learns to return to the lure each time that she is released.

Falcons, whether they are male or female, are referred to as 'her' or 'she'. The female is about a third larger than the male, so is stronger, but the smaller size of the male helps it twist and turn quickly in flight.

In October, falcons arrive on the eastern coast of the Arabian peninsula on their migration routes. A bird is trapped and trained for one hunting season. Then she is released again in the spring. Care must be taken not to damage the falcons when trapping them.

Female   Male

? How are falcons trapped?

There are many different methods used to trap falcons. Here are just two of them.

A net is suspended between two sticks and some sort of live bait, such as a gerbil, is fixed beside the net. The trap is put up in a flimsy way so it collapses easily. The falcon concentrates on seizing the prey and fails to notice the net, which falls down on her and entangles her.

A 'decoy'. A shelter made of brushwood is built over a hole in the sand. A pigeon is used to attract and trap a falcon. The pigeon is pinned to the ground, in a shallow dip edged with stones. A line is attached to the pigeon and the falconer holds the other end of it. There are nylon nooses at the end of the line where it is tied to the pigeon. When a falcon flies down to attack the pigeon, her talons are entangled in the nooses. The falconer then pulls her back to his hide.

A glove, dass or kaff, or a cuff, manqalah, protects the falconer's arm from the bird's sharp talons.

Some young men love to play football. Others are keen on cricket, but for many young men in Arabia there is nothing so thrilling as spending time training and hunting with their falcon.

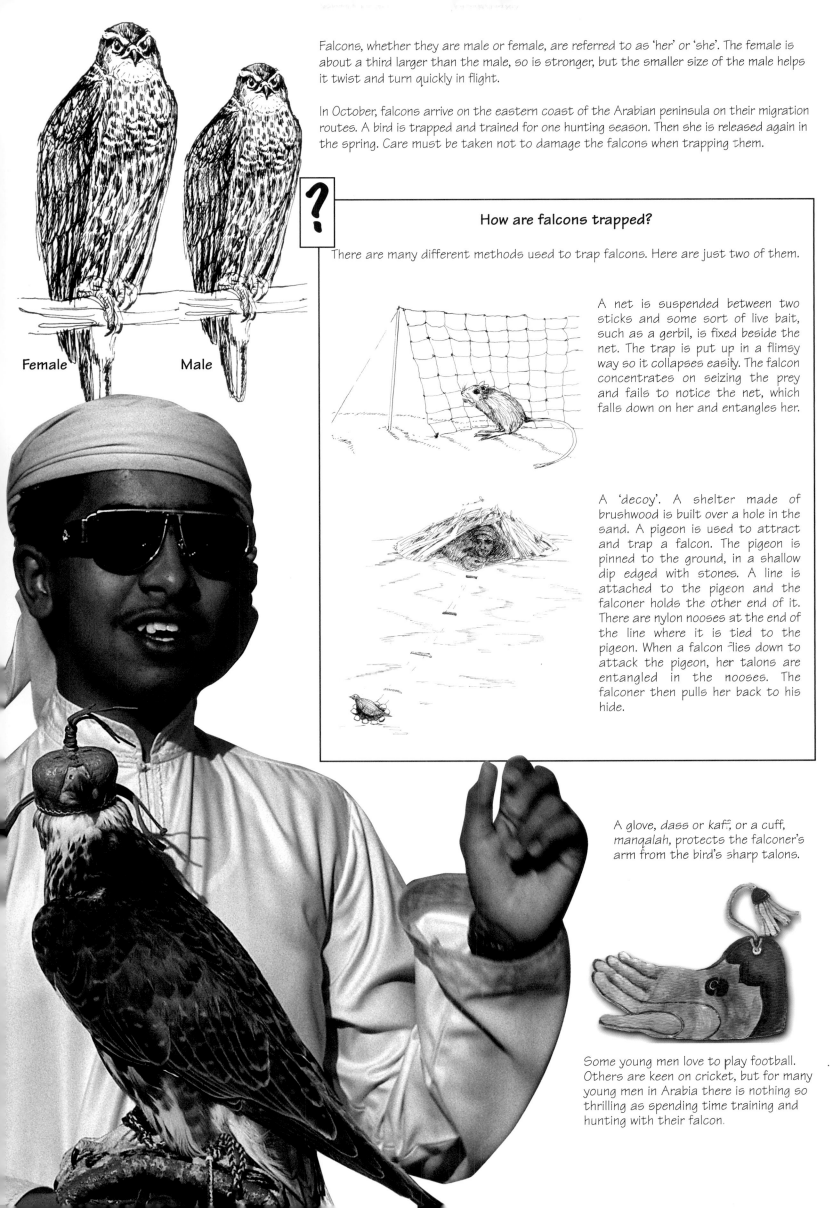

TAKING PART IN FALCONRY

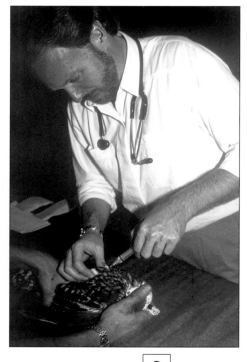

A large group of people enjoy and take part in the art of falcony in many parts of the Arabian peninsula. Young men learn from their fathers how to hunt and the bond of respect and affection between an Arab and his falcon is very strong. Great excitement fills the air as news of a hunt goes round. Everyone looks forward to spending time together. There are opportunities for the sheikhs to spend time with their followers and allegiances between the falconers and their leader are strengthened. However, problems for the sport developed as the traditional quarry declined in numbers. Strong measures had to be taken to control the hunting of the Houbara Bustard, Stone Curlew and Desert Hare. In all the countries of the Arabian peninsula, government decrees were issued to protect them. In some areas they cannot be hunted at all and in others hunting is restricted to small isolated regions. Hunting parties now take place in other countries, such as Pakistan.

Taking care of a falcon and ensuring that she is in good health has always been important to the falconer.

At a falcon hospital, *left*, doctors mend bones, treat diseases and carry out operations in just the same way as on people attending hospital when they are sick. Rare falcons are microchipped to help protect them against theft and record information about the vaccinations given to each one.

Traditional methods of treatment are now combined with the latest modern technology to keep falcons healthy during their time in captivity.

!

FACTOID

Falcons are very expensive to buy. In the bird souq, a beautifully coloured young bird can cost more than $35,000. Specially bred falcons are also bought from Europe and they cost even more than the wild ones that have been trapped.

A falcon waits her turn at the falcon hospital. Her case notes are at her feet recording her medical history.

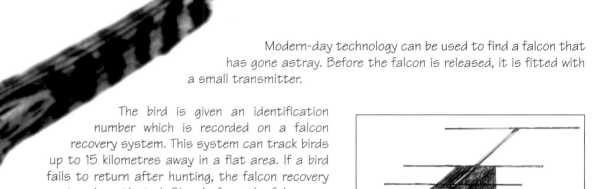

Modern-day technology can be used to find a falcon that has gone astray. Before the falcon is released, it is fitted with a small transmitter.

The bird is given an identification number which is recorded on a falcon recovery system. This system can track birds up to 15 kilometres away in a flat area. If a bird fails to return after hunting, the falcon recovery system is activated. Signals from the falcon are picked up by the recovery system and her position is traced.

What prey does a falconer like to hunt?

Houbara Bustards are the favourite quarry of falconers. They are shy, secretive birds that live in desert habitats. The males perform an extraordinary dance when they are courting the female. Feathers of the head and neck of the male fan out as he attempts to attract the female. Like falcons, they are migratory birds spending the winter months in Arabia. They breed in central Asia. Houbara Bustards have a special aid to defend themselves from a falcon. They squirt out slimey faeces which can temporarily blind the falcon or gum up her feathers.

Houbara Bustard

Governments of the countries that make up the Arabian peninsula have set up organisations to look into the needs of its wildlife. Part of their work has been to study the habitats and migration routes of Peregrine and Saker Falcons, as well as the Houbara Bustard.

The diagram (below) shows the route taken by a Houbara Bustard released in the United Arab Emirates. In travelling to China and back the Houbara Bustard flew 12,300 km.

A tiny transmitter weighing only 34 grams was fitted onto a Houbara Bustard so that it could be tracked by satellite. The Houbara Bustard was then released.

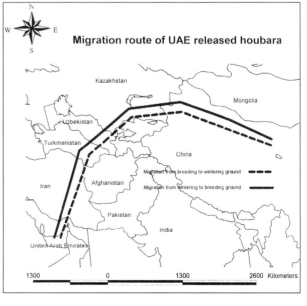

Migration route of UAE released houbara

- Migration from breeding to wintering ground
- Migration from wintering to breeding ground

CAMEL RACING

Camel racing is a sport that is centuries old in Arabia and is part of Bedu culture. The Arabian one-humped camel is called a dromedary which comes from the Greek word *dromeus*, meaning a 'runner'. A dromedary has a lighter skeleton and smaller feet than the two-humped camel and is known for its speed.

Camel races are conducted in all the countries of the Arabian peninsula, encouraged by their rulers, who are keen supporters of racing. The Bedu gather in major cities, where there are large well-organised tracks, or at smaller village celebrations where racing is organised informally. The rulers buy good pedigree camels from the Bedu at the end of each season. Money from the camel sales benefits many members of the community. Racing takes place several times a week throughout the winter months. Camel owners come from many different countries to compete for the important end of season races, sometimes bringing their camels by aeroplane or truck. There is always an atmosphere of great excitement at each event as the camels and their riders race towards the finishing post.

Jockeys have to train every day for racing. Boys must build up their fitness and weigh no more than 30 kilograms. They wear protective helmets, and velcro on the inside of their trousers to help them stay on the camels. Each jockey carries a two-way radio in his pocket, so that his trainer can give him instructions while he is racing. At the end of the season, huge camel carnivals are held in the large cities with prize money of thousands of dollars.

In Qatar, the UAE and Oman, remote-controlled robots are sometimes used instead of jockeys.

Two days before racing, the camel's stomach is purged. Afterwards, the camels is washed and covered with special blankets. It is fed and watered before being covered again. A special hood is placed over its mouth to prevent it eating anything else before the race.

The back of the camel, with its one hump, is an awkward place to sit, but it is more comfortable than sitting behind the neck. The racing saddle is small and light.

For two or three months before the racing season starts a lot of hard work is put into training the camels and jockeys.

Not all camel racing takes place at big city camel tracks. Racing also takes place on Fridays and national holidays between people from neighbouring villages. The races are followed by the camel owners in four-wheel drive vehicles, excitedly encouraging their camels on to victory.

Unlike a horse race which covers a short distance, a camel race is a test of endurance. The tracks are oval, and vary in length from one country to another, but in the Gulf states races of 10 kilometres are the preferred distance. These races are for camels that are 6 years or older. There are shorter tracks of 3, 4 and 5 kilometres for younger camels whose bones are not yet mature. A race on the 10 kilometre track lasts for about 18 minutes.

!

FACTOID

A camel's teeth show its age. A racing camel is grouped, depending on its age. Judges at each racetrack inspect its teeth to decide which race it can go into. Losing one of its teeth, even as it is going round the track, means its age has changed and other competitors can protest about it being in the wrong race.

In Saudi Arabia, the King holds endurance races over 20 kilometres. Up to 7,000 camels may take part, as the winners are those who complete the course not just the one first past the finishing line.

?

How are camels chosen for each race?

Beside the race course is a huge holding pen for all the camels that will enter that day's races. A committee, appointed by the rulers, decides on the races for the day, usually about ten in total. Some races are only for males, others only for females. Races are also divided into age groups. Camels are marked on their neck to show which race they may enter.

THE ARABIAN HORSE

The Arabian horse has existed as a breed for several thousand years and is considered a true, pure bred horse. The Bedu on the Arabian peninsula, who perfected the breed, carefully controlled their bloodlines. The history of every Arab mare was so important to the tribe that the head man knew all the details of each animal as well as he knew the history of his own family. The Bedu considered the horse a gift from God, created from mist and dust. They treated it with the love and respect that such a precious gift deserved. The mares were given affection like a member of the family. This early contact with family life has bred a gentle and affectionate nature in Arabian horses. Their courage and speed was important to the survival of the tribe during raiding parties. If the raid went badly, a good horse ensured a safe get-away for its rider. The qualities of the Arabian horse have created a breed that is just as highly valued today as it was in the past. Studs, where they are bred, have been set up in all parts of the world.

Arab

Thoroughbred

> And God took a handful of South wind and from it formed a horse saying:
> "I create thee, Oh Arabian. To thy forelock, I bind Victory in battle.
> On thy back, I set a rich spoil and a Treasure in thy loins.
> I establish thee as one of the Glories of the Earth...
> I give thee flight without wings."
>
> **From an ancient Bedouin legend**

All Thoroughbreds descend from the original stock of three Arab stallions: the Byerley Turk; the Darley Arabian; and the Godolphin Arabian. Thoroughbreds are the world's supreme racehorses, being strong and powerful with tremendous stamina.

Many Arab leaders are skilled and knowledgeable racehorse owners who have played a part in the international horse world since the 1970s.

The appearance of the Arabian horse is quite unmistakable. The number of ribs and lumbar vertebrae differs between the Arabian and other horses.

The formation of the short back and muscular hind quarters with the tail carried high are unique to the Arabian horse.

The Arabian usually stands between 14 and 15.2 hands high.

Tail carried high

Short back

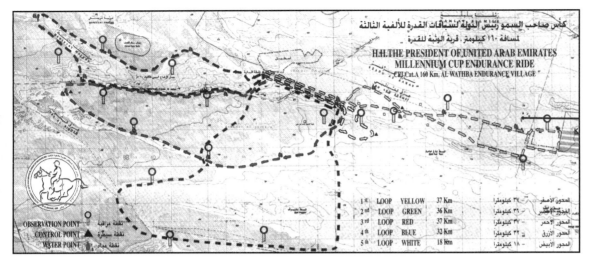

The Arabian horse has always been prized for its endurance. Endurance racing has been re-introduced into the United Arab Emirates, Qatar and Bahrain. In the first races, held in 1993, both horses and camels took part.

It was thought that the camels would win, but the horses easily outstripped them. An endurance race takes place over a long distance. No swapping of horses is allowed. Each horse with just one rider must complete the whole route.

An endurance race takes place over a series of loops. At the end of each loop the horse must be presented for a veterinary inspection within 30 minutes of arrival. Riders enter the control point using a magnetic swipe card, which eliminates manual timings. After the condition of the horse has been checked, there is a 'hold time', which is a compulsory rest period of 20-40 minutes before the race can be re-joined. Big prizes are awarded to the winners. $400,000 was given in prize money for the United Arab Emirates Millennium Cup. Riders come from all over the world to compete. Each horse has a passport, issued by the Equestrian Federation. This identifies it, and records its age and health.

The Dubai World Cup

FACTOID

Prize money for the Dubai World Cup is $6,000,000. It is the richest race in the world. It was first run in 1995 and is now a Group 1 race, which recognises the highest standard of horses competing and the fine facilities of the race track.

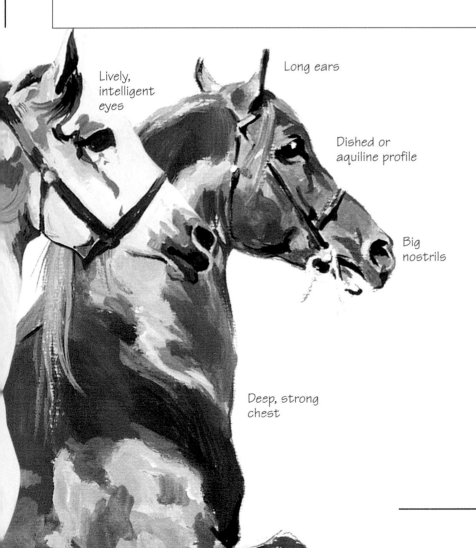

Lively, intelligent eyes

Long ears

Dished or aquiline profile

Big nostrils

Deep, strong chest

The popularity of horse racing has achieved great heights in Arabia. Racing is held several times a week during the winter months at the first class race-courses around the Arabian peninsula. The horses are moved to stables in Europe and the United States for the summer.

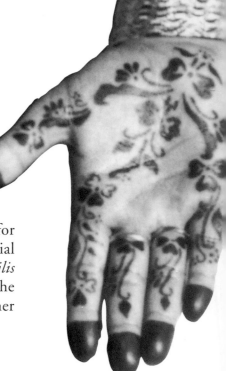

The people of Arabia are well known for the welcome they give their guests. Visits are considered happy occasions and much time and thought is put into making the home ready to receive guests. The hostess plans the food depending on the arrival time of her guests. Then she burns incense and prepares bottles of various perfumes to offer her guests. She chooses a beautiful dress, embroidered with silver or gold thread, to wear. Her hands and feet are decorated with henna, which is used for decoration and for its medicinal properties. Men and women do not mix on social occasions. When guests arrive, the family breaks into two groups. The men eat in the *majlis* with the host and the women in the living room with the hostess. The last task of the hostess is to bring around the perfume after the meal. When the guests have enjoyed her choice of fragrances, it is time for everyone to depart.

A woman blends her own perfumes, and keeps the ingredients secret. Some of the different oils used are very expensive, but a woman is proud to be known as someone who uses the best.

The most important ingredient of both perfumes and incense is Aloewood, known as oudh, which grows in India. Its price varies depending on its quality but it can be very expensive – the best costs $6,000 a kilo.

Most of the oils come from plants. Saffron, oudh and rose oil are popular but there are many different oils to choose from. Oils are sold in small bottles. After being blended, the perfume is put in the dark for forty days. This improves its quality.

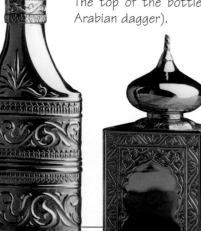

!

FACTOID

Amouage, made in Oman, is among the most expensive perfumes in the world. One of its ingredients is so pure it is called silver frankincense. The top of the bottle is shaped like a *khanjar* (an Arabian dagger).

Getting ready to celebrate special days, such as weddings, national days or the *Eid* holidays is an important part of the occasion. Hands are beautifully decorated and new dresses made. From the time she is a young child, an Arab girl will have her own pieces of jewellery for special occasions.

Designs of jewellery vary in diferent regions of the Arabian peninsula but necklaces, hair ornaments, bracelets and rings are worn everywhere. A murtasha, a necklace, can be short or so long it almost reaches the waist. The word murtash means trembling, and describes the movement of the beads around the neck.

Where does henna come from?

The leaves of the henna tree (*below*) are gathered and laid on a tray to dry. Then they are pounded into a fine powder. Sometimes boiled lime juice is added to the henna making it just wet enough to be kneaded into a thick paste. Henna leaves, dried powder and even ready-mixed paste can be bought in the shops.

Henna is traditionally used to improve health. Painting the soles of the feet is a way of insulating them from the hot sand. Henna is also said to prevent eye sores and headaches. It is used to make hair shiny and free of dandruff.

The night before her wedding a bride has her hands and feet decorated with henna. She stays quietly in her room, as it is believed that if the bride is seen before her marriage day her face will lose its beauty.

Traditional Bedouin designs

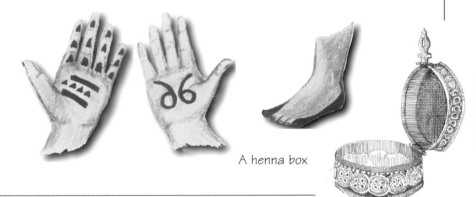

A henna box

How is incense made?

Small brown cakes of incense called *dukhan* or *bakhoor* are made from *oudh* wood, ground up into a powder with various oils.

Ambergris is used to bind the incense cakes together. A spoonful of sugar is added before the cakes are put into a dark place to dry for two months. They are then ready to be used.

Small chips of *oudh* wood (*below*) are put onto burning charcoals. A thick fragrant smoke arises from the wood chips as they burn.

A trader weighs the *oudh* in the *souq*.

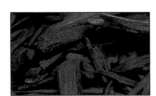

The incense cakes are broken into small pieces and dug into the embers of the charcoal. The incense burner is passed round amongst the guests, to perfume their clothes and body.

A traditional incense burner.

CLOTHING

Although the Arabian peninsula is made up of seven separate countries, the style of clothing in the cities is similar. Outside the cities, there is more variation in traditional dress. Rich materials of brilliant colours are used by both men and women, often embroidered with silver thread. Over the centuries, trade with distant lands has influenced the Arabian style of dress. The people's religion, Islam, requires both men and women to be modestly dressed. It is the practice to cover the entire body, and in some countries this includes the face. The climate also affects what people wear to protect themselves from the hot sun, harsh wind or swirling sands. Today, most women in cities wear brightly-coloured dresses combining traditional and modern styles, which they cover with a loose black cloak when they leave the house. For men, the normal outfit is a long white garment called a *dishdasha* or *thobe*, and on their heads a *ghoutra* – a square of white or red-and-white checked material worn in a variety of styles.

?

What would men wear on their heads?

Though popular with men and boys throughout the region, the red-and-white checked *shemagh* is also worn as military headdress in some regiments. The Bedu were said to go into battle with their shemagh wrapped tightly round their faces so they could not be recognised.

Hats woven from palm fronds are worn by workers in the fields to protect them from the sun. They are typical of the Yemen and southern Saudi Arabia.

The headcloth can be fashioned into a variety of styles. It is neat and stays securely on the head.

On formal and ceremonial occasions a *bisht* of fine silk, or wool is worn. Usually black or cinnamon coloured, it is edged with pure gold thread. The white *ghoutra* is held in place with a twisted black coil called an *'iqal* – literally, a tethering rope.

An embroidered cap called a *kuma* is often worn in Oman. Holes are pierced in the material and beige or white threads carefully stitched round them, forming intricate patterns.

This gathering of men and boys shows the variety of ways the headdress can be worn.

What would women traditionally wear?

Women's clothes are never revealing and hair is always covered. The different styles can show to which community a woman belongs. Although traditional styles vary, a dress, or *kandoora*, with tight-fitting arms is usually worn under a lacy or embroidered *thobe*, over a pair of trousers.

These young Omani girls are dressed in their best clothes for the *Eid* holiday celebrations. Bright colours are still worn in rural areas as everyday dress, and women are not veiled.

A wedding guest from the Asir region of Saudi Arabia.

In Saudi Arabia and the countries bordering the Arabian Gulf it is usual to see women wearing a veil in public.

Traditionally clothes were stored in woven bags or chests (above), which were often the most important item of furniture in the home. They were given to brides on their wedding day and filled with new clothes and bed linen.

CELEBRATIONS AND MUSIC

The sounds of songs and drumming fill the air. Men with camel sticks, swords or rifles are gathering together to celebrate their happiness. The occasion may be a religious holiday such as *Eid* or a marriage in the community. Traditional dances accompanied by poetry take part in every region of the Arabian peninsula. The words may be from well-known sources or they may be new and improvised as the dance progresses. They are an essential part of the dance. Women have their own dances, often performed in two rows, moving backwards and forwards in time to the beat. African and Asian rhythms can be heard in the music brought to Arabia by travellers and traders over the centuries. In the past, music also accompanied occupational activities. Moving rhythmically and chanting together made long, hard work pass more easily. The Bedu have their own repertoire of chants which are sometimes romantic, dwelling on their memories or reflecting the harsh environment of the desert.

Marriages are celebrated over several days with feasting and entertainment among the family and friends of the bride and groom. Traditionally, marriage occurs between cousins. A bride price, paid by the bridegroom, is agreed and a date for the wedding set. Bridal gifts from the husband to his wife become her property. After a marriage contract is signed, wedding festivities begin.

The Yemeni men above are dressed in traditional wedding costume, their headdresses gaily adorned with flowers and herbs.

?

What would be served for a favourite wedding meal?

A wedding, or other festive occasion when many people are entertained, calls for a very special meal. A whole goat is cooked in a specially prepared oven called a shuwa. A pit is dug about one metre deep. It is lined with stones, which are heated until they are white-hot by burning wood in the pit.

The goat is cut into large pieces and marinated in a mixture of spices. Many spices are used, such as cumin, coriander, pepper and tumeric. Fresh ginger, tamarind juice, lime juice and salt are also added. Finally, the goat is covered in a cloth and wrapped in banana and date leaves. It is lowered into the pit, which is then covered by a lid. Earth is piled on top of the lid.

The whole dish takes about 24 hours to cook and results in a delicious meal.

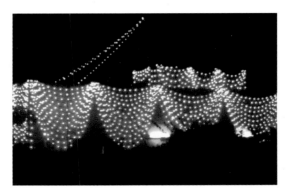

A house decked out with lights announces that a weddingparty is taking place.

What kind of musical instruments are used in celebration?

A skirt of goat hooves was fixed around the waist. It rattled rhythmically as the dancer moved from side to side.

In Saudi Arabia the men (*below*) gather for a dignified but spirited traditional dance to the powerful beat of the drums.

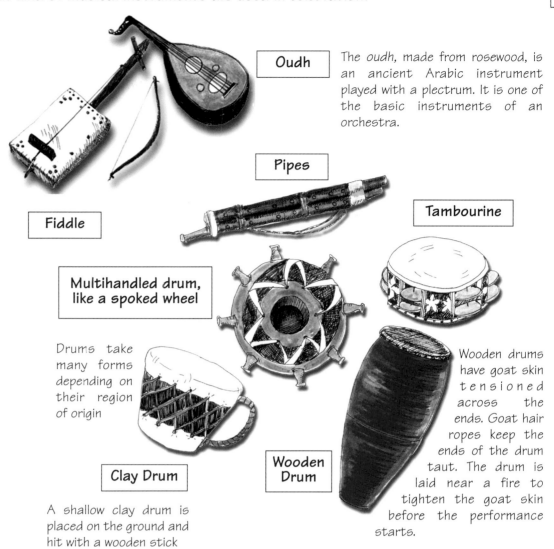

Oudh

The *oudh*, made from rosewood, is an ancient Arabic instrument played with a plectrum. It is one of the basic instruments of an orchestra.

Pipes

Fiddle

Tambourine

Multihandled drum, like a spoked wheel

Drums take many forms depending on their region of origin

Clay Drum

A shallow clay drum is placed on the ground and hit with a wooden stick

Wooden Drum

Wooden drums have goat skin tensioned across the ends. Goat hair ropes keep the ends of the drum taut. The drum is laid near a fire to tighten the goat skin before the performance starts.

FLORA AND
FAUNA

Deserts are areas of very little rainfall. They can either be hot, as in Arabia, or cold, as in Antarctica. A hot desert is one of the harshest places in the world to live. In the summer the sun burns down relentlessly. During the hottest months, temperatures reach more than 50°C and everything that lives there struggles to survive. Rain only falls during the winter, so for a few short months plants hurry to produce their seeds and animals to have their young, before the heat returns once more. The Arabian peninsula has a wide variety of scenery and habitats. Deserts are not only sandy dunes, but flat gravel plains. High barren mountains and deep river beds, known as wadis, also provide different features of the Arabian landscape. Mountains cause some rain to fall but it quickly runs away down the wadi beds. Very clever ways to overcome the arid conditions have been developed by the plants and creatures that make a desert their home.

Caracal tracks

How are sand dunes formed?

Sand dunes are formed from small particles of stone carried by the wind. The wind can only lift grains of sand about 1 metre off the ground so when an obstacle is in its way, such as a tree, the sand drops to the ground. Eventually the sand dune itself is an obstacle and more sand gets dropped on it.

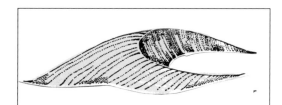

Crescent shaped dunes are known as barchans. They are formed when the wind comes mostly from one direction and there is little sand, such as on the edge of the desert.

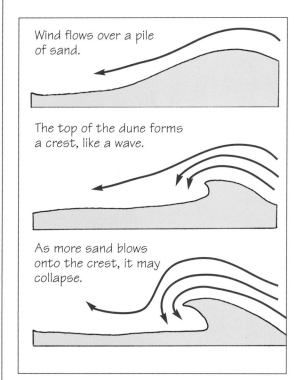

Wind flows over a pile of sand.

The top of the dune forms a crest, like a wave.

As more sand blows onto the crest, it may collapse.

Transverse dunes are formed in areas where there is plenty of sand. Wind blowing from only one direction causes dunes to form at right angles to the wind.

The Desert Rose
Crystals of mineral gypsum form together under a layer of sabkha, the salty flats near the sea, to make these beautiful flower-like shapes.

FACTOID

Some of the largest deserts in the world are in Arabia. At 647,500 square miles, the Rub al Khali, known as the Empty Quarter, is one of the most difficult deserts to cross safely. Only after spring rains, when some grazing had sprung up for the camels to eat, was it possible for the Bedu to journey across its dangerous sand dunes.

Which creatures can live in the desert?

A huge variety of creatures are able to live in desert conditions. This desert beetle has a downwards pointing body. Moisture runs down its back and provides it with all the moisture it needs.

A lizard (*left*) peers out from his sandy hideaway.

Tracks in the sand

The early morning light shows hundreds of tracks criss-crossing the sand. Many desert creatures only emerge at night when it is cool. The Bedu are experts at reading tracks in the sand. They can tell which creatures have passed by and many details about each of them from its footprints. They use tracks to find out which direction has been taken by members of other tribes and whether a person was alone or with others. It is essential to their survival to understand clues that tracks provide.

One small shrimp-like animal, Tricopsgranarius (*left*), lays eggs that develop into hard cysts when pools in the desert dry up. They lie buried in the sand, sometimes for many years. When rain falls, the embryo shrimp emerges from the cyst, quickly grows to adult size and itself reproduces eggs. After a short time the pools disappear once more and the eggs lie unnoticed in the sand waiting for another rain shower.

Rain falling in the mountains rushes down the wadi beds with great force. Moisture continues to lie in pools between the rocks and just below the surface of the gravel, even when the wadi has dried out. Many creatures and plants are to be found in these habitats.

CAMELS — MASTERS OF ADAPTATION

The camel is the first animal that comes to mind when we think about creatures that have adapted to life in the desert. They are members of the family called *Camelidae*. Camels originated in North America and migrated westwards across Alaska to Eastern Asia and Africa, when the land masses were still joined. These animals were no larger than hares. As they settled in Asia they separated into two groups. Gradually they developed into the two different types of camel we know today – the Arabian camel (called a dromedary), which had one hump, and the Bactrian camel, which has two humps.

Other members of the Camelidae family are llamas, vicunas, alpacas and guanacos, which moved southwards to South America, developing very different characteristics as they adapted to the mountainous terrain and cold climate.

Before the arrival of motorised transport on the Arabian peninsula, the camel was essential for any journey. Its ability to survive without water for long periods and to walk across sand without sinking in made it the only animal suitable for desert travel. Even now, the Bedouin rely on the camel, not only for transport but for its milk, its hair and hide for making belts, waterskins and saddles. The she-camel is normally used for riding and the male camel for carrying baggage.

Camels thrive in arid areas where the vegetation is sparse. In the winter there is plenty of fodder, but in summer the plants are dry and scarce. A camel can get nourishment from almost any plant.

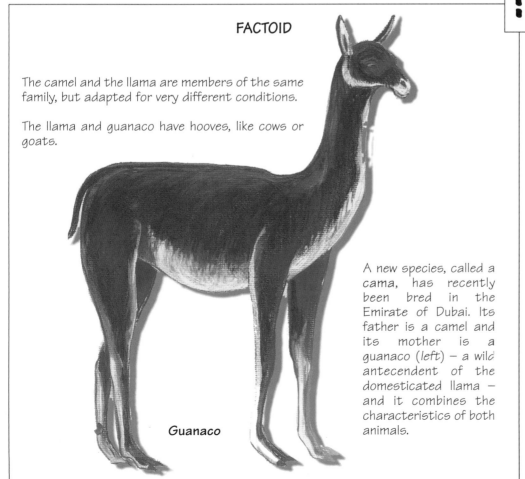

!

FACTOID

The camel and the llama are members of the same family, but adapted for very different conditions.

The llama and guanaco have hooves, like cows or goats.

Guanaco

A new species, called a cama, has recently been bred in the Emirate of Dubai. Its father is a camel and its mother is a guanaco (*left*) – a wild antecedent of the domesticated llama – and it combines the characteristics of both animals.

!

FACTOID

A camel's foot has only two toes but it is made for walking on sand. A pad of fat between the toes spreads the foot out flat, so that it doesn't sink in.

An extra joint in their foot helps them climb up very steep sand dunes.

Acacia trees (*above and in the background right*) are one of the camel's favourite meals. The trees show a marked line across the bottom edge of their branches, where the camel has eaten the leaves and twigs.

In the heat of the day, the camel will lie facing into the sun so less of its body area is exposed to direct sunlight.

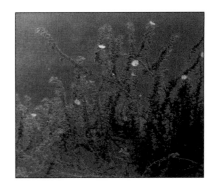

On the ground, tribulus (*above*) and dipterygium are favourite meals. When nothing else is available, the camel will eat bitter and salty plants which are avoided by other animals grazing in the desert.

Ears are set back on their heads and covered with hair inside and out.

A camel's teeth are very sharp, enabling it to bite off hard, prickly parts of desert trees. However, it does not devour the branches or spines. Its sensitive lips avoid the sharp thorns, working round and between them to strip off the tender leaves.

Each eye is protected by long eyelashes to keep the sand out. They also have a third eyelid, which washes and cleans the cornea.

Their slit-shaped nostrils can close completely to stop sand getting into their air-passages.

Low grazing

The owner will sometimes put a bag over the camel's nose and mouth to stop it eating unsavoury things.

Camels have hard pads on their knees and stomach. These pads protect their legs when they kneel and raise the stomach slightly off the sand, helping to keep them cool.

REDUCE SPEED NOW

The camel has not adapted well to the coming of the motor car. Its reflexes are quite slow, and it has no road sense. Fences and signs have been erected to warn motorists. A collision with a camel can be fatal to both parties.

High browsing

DESERT MAMMALS — CHAMPIONS OF WATER CONSERVATION

Creatures that live in desert conditions adapt in many ways to help them in their struggle to get water and prevent it escaping from their bodies. When a camel has been starved of water for long periods, it is able to take in huge quantities at one time and rehydrate itself quickly. It is possible for a camel to drink 115 litres of water in one day. It is said that a camel can survive for about 30 days without drinking water, but that depends on the time of year, and whether the grazing is good. It is possible for the camel to get 30 litres of water from the plants it eats each day when the conditions are good. Nowadays, camels seen wandering around the desert are not wild. Camels are branded with a special mark called a *wasm* to show who they belong to.

The camel has very efficient kidneys. It passes little urine in hot weather in order not to lose water. Its kidneys also allow it to drink salty or bitter water that our kidneys would not be able to cope with. Its dung is also very dry and is used by the Bedu to make fires.

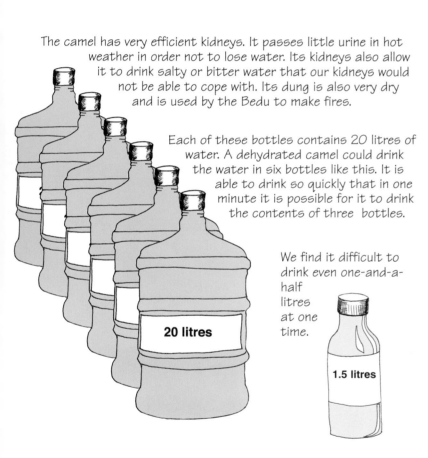

Each of these bottles contains 20 litres of water. A dehydrated camel could drink the water in six bottles like this. It is able to drink so quickly that in one minute it is possible for it to drink the contents of three bottles.

20 litres

We find it difficult to drink even one-and-a-half litres at one time.

1.5 litres

The hump of a camel consists almost entirely of fat. Camels do not store water in their humps. If food is short, the hump can provide energy for the camel. In a starving camel the hump shrinks but it will become plump again when the camel is fed.

Camels are able to control their body temperature. They are not harmed if their body temperature rises from 34.5°C in the morning to 40.5°C in the afternoon. If our temperature rises by only one or two degrees we feel ill. The camel's temperature is brought down again at night, when it is cool. It doesn't waste much water by sweating.

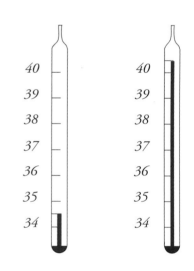

Temperature in degrees celsius

Man is not nearly as well adapted to desert conditions. In hot temperatures, he can lose as much as 4 litres of water an hour cooling his body.

The Natural History Museum in the Emirate of Sharjah has a mechanical camel! It is a fun way to show some of the camel's adaptations to desert life.

What special blood cooling methods help survival in the desert?

The oryx is truly adapted to life in the desert, and does not need a source of fresh water to drink. It relies on water in its food and moisture from cool night air.

At night, moisture from sea fogs rolls across the desert. It is deposited on plants and fur of the desert animals. The oryx licks this moisture to increase its water intake.

All the antelope family have long nasal passages to cool down the hot air they breathe.

This diagram of the oryx shows how the nasal passages are thought to help in bringing down the temperature in the blood going to its brain.

1. Blood containing oxygen is carried by arteries from the heart to the brain. This blood is hot and would kill the oryx if it entered the brain at this temperature.

2. A special adaptation prevents the hot blood from from entering the brain. Instead it enters a network of small vessels from the carotid arteries.

3. There the blood is cooled by the evaporation of moisture in the oryx's nostrils. The blood that enters the brain is up to three degrees cooler than the blood in the rest of its body.

Blood entering the brain

In a network of small vessels blood from the carotid arteries is cooled.

Hot oxygenated blood from the heart.

Blood cooling in the veins of the nostrils.

All desert mammals are lighter and smaller than similar creatures in colder parts of the world. For instance, a desert fox is smaller than a European fox.

The fur on some desert mammals is surprisingly long and thick, particularly on the feet. This protects them from the hot sand. Fur and feathers are also poor conductors of heat, so they slow down hot air from reaching their bodies.

Cape hare

The large surface area of the Cape hare's ears helps to cool its blood. Unlike rabbits, the hare does not live in a burrow. It scrapes out small cave-like shelters from the sand. It relies on speed to escape its predators, so the leverets (young hares) are capable of running when they are born. They have fur and are not blind and helpless like baby rabbits.

The toes of a Lesser jerboa have tufts of stiff hair.

DESERT MAMMALS — DIET AND SURVIVAL

For desert mammals life is a battle for moisture. They must balance the amount of water that they need to survive with the amount of water lost from their bodies. Water is lost by any activity, particularly moving around in the heat. Even breathing causes loss of water. If too much water is lost an animal's body fluids, such as blood, become too concentrated and the creature dies. Many animals adapt by taking time out from the heat. They can do this in two ways. One is by going into a torpor, or state of sleepiness. In cool sheltered homes underneath the sand, their body temperature drops until they become comatose and can sleep for many hours without waking. The second way to escape the heat is to use night hours for activity. At dusk, creatures come out of their burrows and holes to take advantage of cool temperatures and to feed.

The rare Ruppell's sand fox stays underground during the day. It comes out at night to feed on a diet of small mammals and birds.

?

What do these groups of animals like to eat?

Carnivores are meat eaters. Their bodies are specially adapted for hunting live prey. They have well-developed brains, and claws at the end of their toes. They have powerful teeth and a flesh tooth at the front of their jaw for tearing meat.

Tahr

Indian grey mongoose

Herbivores eat plants. Their teeth are arranged so they can pull at leaves and grasses. The back teeth then chew their food.

Skull of a mongoose

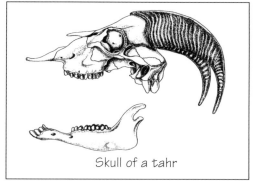
Skull of a tahr

Honey badger

Some animals like many different kinds of foods. They are omnivores. Because meat is part of their diet they have the same large front teeth as the carnivores.

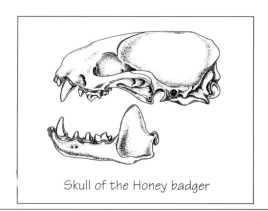
Skull of the Honey badger

FACTOID

Yellow eyes or brown eyes? Although wild dogs and wolves look very similar, the way to tell them apart is by the colour of their eyes. A true wolf has golden eyes, but the dog's eyes are dark brown. Wolves are almost extinct in Arabia now.

The eyes of a wolf

The eyes of a dog

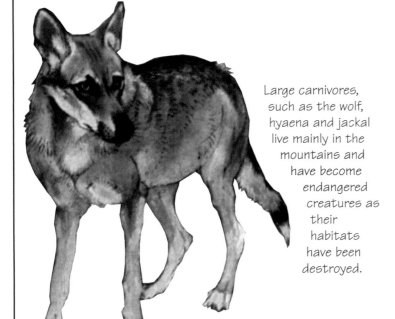

Large carnivores, such as the wolf, hyaena and jackal live mainly in the mountains and have become endangered creatures as their habitats have been destroyed.

Arabian wolf

The Striped hyaena

The Striped hyaena has a heavy dog-like build. It feeds largely on carrion (dead meat left by other hunters) but also hunts for its food. Its powerful teeth enable it to break up large bones.

The Blanford's fox (*below*) is also a mountain dweller and is well camouflaged by its dark grey colour against the rocky terrain. It has remarkable hearing and its large ears are able to pick up sounds of insects burrowing below the ground.

However, the Blanford's fox does not only rely on meat for its diet. It is also happy to eat fruit. It is fond of the fruit of the *sidr* tree (*right*) when it is in season and this can make up to 90 per cent of its diet.

Foxes produce two to three young each year.

Blanford's fox

The Red fox (*below*) is the most successful of the foxes, and their numbers are high in all areas. It is content to live close to humans, scavenging from rubbish tips. It is much larger and faster than the other two species of fox and is known to hunt them, as well as goats and sheep, small birds, reptiles and rodents. On the coast, foxes catch fish to eat.

Red fox

DESERT MAMMALS — SMALL CREATURES

Many small creatures inhabit rock crevices, holes and caves in the desert habitat. They are the prey of other animals and birds but they are fast moving and agile, as they dart between boulders or their holes in the sand. As well as having many adaptations to cope with the climate, they rely on their large numbers to survive. They are under constant attack from predators but they breed rapidly. They have many babies at one time and the babies grow up quickly. They can produce babies only a few weeks after being born themselves. This helps replace the many animals that are eaten daily. They are successful survivors in every kind of environment that the desert provides.

Cheesman's gerbil

What type of rodents live in the desert?

The word 'rodent' means 'gnawing animal'. They have a long pair of front teeth in each jaw which keep growing. As the animal bites on his diet of hard seeds, the teeth wear down.

This group includes rats, mice, jerboas, gerbils, jirds, hamsters, and voles.

Spiny mouse

The nocturnal Spiny mouse has an unusual tail which can easily break off at the end, leaving an enemy with only a small piece of the mouse as it escapes to safety. Also its prickly fur makes it difficult for an enemy to swallow it.

A female Spiny mouse can produce babies when she is just 31 days old. She has between two and five young every time she gives birth.

The jerboa is a one of the creatures best adapted to desert life. Much of its time is spent collecting food from far and wide. It hides seeds in sandy burrows and in times of intense heat it goes into a sleepy state called aestivating. The burrow is sealed with an earth plug. This is a 'time out' method of reducing all activity.

Arabian lesser jerboa

The jerboa has small front legs, but strong back ones. It moves in acrobatic jumps. It can leap 70 centimetres into the air from a standing position helped by its long tail which is uses to balance itself.

The gerbils

There are several different species of gerbil, and the rat-like gerbils known as jirds, throughout Arabia.

Most gerbils and jirds live together in a colony with many other members of their group. They build warrens of underground tunnels.

The tail of the Fat jird is much shorter than the Bushy-tailed jird. It constructs large warrens and feeds on juicy desert plants. It gets its water from the foliage of plants.

The Bushy-tailed jird is a rat-like gerbil. More than half its size is taken up by its tail which has fur extending all the way down it to a tuft on the end.

Fat jird

The pale sandy colouring of the shy, nocturnal Cheesman's gerbil (*left*) camouflages it perfectly against its desert habitat. The soles of its feet are hairy and hundreds of tracks can be seen in the sand every morning showing that gerbils have been busy throughout the night.

Cheesman's gerbils enjoy seeds of the desert squash (*right*) which are poisonous to many other animals.

Desert squash

The largest of the rodents is the Porcupine.

Unlike other rodents, the porcupine cannot escape its enemies by fleeing. It relies on its razor sharp quills, raising them defensively if attacked. Its short tail is armed with a cluster of special 'rattling quills'. The ends of these are wide and hollow to make a threatening noise.

When attacked, it charges backwards at its enemy inflicting deep wounds with its spines, which may become stuck in the flesh of its attacker.

It is considered a delicacy by the Bedu

Porcupine

?

Which animals live on insects?

Brandt's hedgehog

Hedgehogs have spiny bristles like the porcupine but they are not part of the same family. Hedgehogs are insectivores. Their long snouts are used for digging up their diet of insects and grubs. They have many small pointed teeth.

The body of a baby hedgehog is pink and hairless when it is born. The spines are soft and white. In four weeks its body has grown hair, and the spines become prickly and darker in colour.

Rolling itself into a ball is its way of defending itself, so that only its prickly back shows. However, it is able to run surprisingly fast.

Brandt's hedgehog. This rare and little known species (*above*) is thought to have come to Arabia across the land bridge from Iran and southern Russia.

The Ethiopian hedgehog (*right*) is able to survive in the true desert. Like other animals that are totally adapted to desert life, it is not necessary for it to drink water regularly. Its diet provides it with all the water it needs.

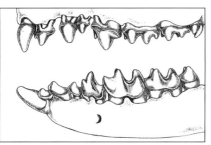
Skull of an Ethiopian hedgehog

High rocky mountains, seas of sand, village oases and cities – all these places on the Arabian peninsula provide homes for desert mammals. Each of these environments has its own eco-system. An eco-system is a community of plants and animals that depend on each other for their survival. When one of the parts of the eco-system fails, all the other members have a hard time to survive. Scientists study the eco-system of an area to decide whether the environment is healthy for animal life. Many eco-systems in a desert environment are fragile. Life is always a struggle there because of the difficult climate. If it is made more difficult because of man's activities, such as constant traffic over the desert, a whole eco-system can be destroyed.

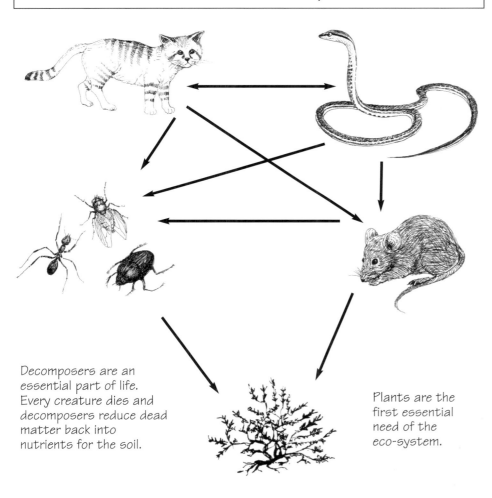

Food web showing how the creatures depend on each other

Decomposers are an essential part of life. Every creature dies and decomposers reduce dead matter back into nutrients for the soil.

Plants are the first essential need of the eco-system.

FACTOID

Saudi Arabia has colonies of baboons that live along the highways in the south-west. They are the only monkeys in Arabia. They sometimes leave their wild habitat and scavenge food from rubbish bins which makes them a nuisance. People are asked not to feed them.

Baboons

Rock hyrax

The Rock hyrax is a nocturnal creature, living on leaves, roots, bulbs, berries and seeds which are the first stage in a food web. The Rock hyrax scurries over the rocky habitat. It has no tail and its blunt toes are like small hooves. Its skeleton proves its ancestry is similar to the elephant and dugong.

Bats feed on insects at night and are among the most mysterious of the night creatures. They are the only mammal that can truly fly. Their wings are delicate membranes extending from their very long forearms, down the sides of their bodies and enclosing their hind limbs and tails.

There are several species of the Leaf-nosed bat. They have a large noseleaf covering their muzzle which enables them to use echolocation to fly in the darkest of caves. Sometimes they roost in the falaj systems.

The Horseshoe bat (left) is a close relative of the Leaf-nosed bat living in caves and dark ruins. Its highly developed powers of echolocation enable it to fly in pitch darkness.

Echolocation means using sound to find things. Creatures that use echolocation do not rely on their eyesight to 'see' things, but measure the time taken for sounds to travel to an object and then bounce off it. The bat's ears, and in some cases the noseleaf as well, are used to pick up the echoes.

Horseshoe bat

Mouse-tailed bats

The Egyptian Fruit bat is a large bat, usually found living in caves and old buildings. It is a nuisance in fruit-growing areas where colonies of the bats feast on bananas, dates, figs and other soft fruit. Its wingspan is more than 30 cm.

Egyptian Fruit bat

Mouse-tailed bats have long tails. They live in large groups, making loud metallic squeaking noises as they fly. Each ear has a tragus which is a piece of prominent flesh at the entrance to the ear canal which helps them pick up sounds.

?

Which animals scavenge off the remains of food?

Some creatures are scavengers, eating the left-over remains of other creatures' food. They are useful as they clear away unwanted rubbish. They fit into the food web as decomposers.

House mouse

Rats live in the cities on rubbish but they also destroy stores of food. The rat family are immigrants to the Arabian peninsula, probably brought in by ships. They can be found in the underground channels of the falaj systems. They bring disease to man so are very unpopular.

Rat

The House mouse is a common creature throughout the area and is one of the smallest rodents. It usually lives in towns and gardens. It becomes a nuisance when it spoils food in people's homes. It also lives in the wild, sharing burrows with other desert rodents, and feeds on seeds and plant roots.

ENDANGERED MAMMALS

For many creatures it has become particularly difficult to survive in the Arabian peninsula. Since the discovery of oil, the environment has become noisier, more crowded and more polluted. Wildlife has been put under pressure, and some species squeezed out by many different problems affecting their habitats. When the known numbers of a species drop below 5,000 they are said to be endangered. Large mammals of Arabia urgently need help to survive before they become extinct. Fortunately, the countries of the Arabian peninsula are aware that these creatures need protection. Land has been allocated for wildlife reserves in some areas. Teams of rangers have been recruited from the local population to gather information about the animals, explain their importance to people and prevent poachers from killing endangered animals.

Caracal

? How do we know when cats are around?

Members of the cat family are nocturnal and very rarely seen. Their footprints are often the clearest signs that they are active.

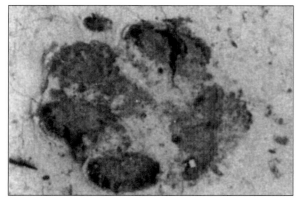

Droppings are an excellent source of information. Although droppings remain on the ground for several months it is easy to tell the age of a dropping, so information can be gained about how recently the animal was in the area.

Scratch marks on trees or rocks tell that a member of the cat family is in the area. Animals mark out their territory with scratch marks and scent it with urine.

Other signs of the presence of creatures in the desert include:

bones and skin from a *dhub* lizard

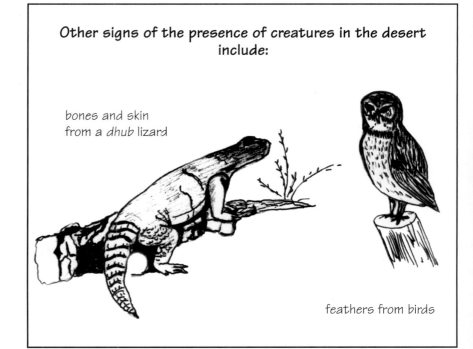

feathers from birds

FACTOID!

The only place in the world where the Tahr lives is in Arabia. High up in the mountains, it runs nimbly on steep rock faces where no other animal can get a foothold.

In 1976 hunting of the Tahr was banned in Oman. Results of a survey completed in 1978 showed there were probably fewer than 2,000 Tahrs left. Rangers made sure that the no hunting rule was enforced and people were punished if they killed the Tahr. Twenty years later the numbers of Tahr appear to be increasing well in many areas, but with new threats to their habitat it is too early to say if they are out of danger.

The Tahr's diet of leaves and fruit is similar to a goat's and it covers great distances in its search for food. The Tahr lives in family groups of three or four animals, and females only give birth to one kid at a time. However, if there has been plenty of rain and the grazing is good, it may have a second kid later in the year.

The Tahr needs to drink fresh water every three or four days in the summer, often coming down at night to drink from springs that feed gardens.

There are few large mammals left in the mountains to prey on the Tahr. The greatest threat to their survival comes from goats. Goats overgraze the vegetation. In the past, shepherds looked after their herds of goats and did not let them roam alone in the highest mountains.

Nowadays not many people want to be shepherds and so the goats are often left to run wild, leaving no food for the Tahr.

Rangers are appointed to keep watch over the animals livingin protected areas.

Every ranger must be prepared to:

Visit local people to explain the importance of protecting animals and gather information.

Pack up supplies of rice, tinned fish, dried shark meat and dates for long nights in the jebel. Water is stored in a goatskin bag. A boulder acts as a table and a mountain ledge a bed.

Travel for as many as three days and nights on patrol, tracking and spotting wild animals. Keep a watch out for poisonous vipers. A slip could be fatal.

Take on duty at nights and weekends when poachers are often active. Investigate information about illegal activities so that the police can take action.

Being a ranger can be a dangerous job.

Rangers on patrol in the high jebel.

ENDANGERED MAMMALS – CATS AND WOLVES

Large animals that hunt for their food, the carnivores, were often seen as enemies by people who kept livestock. The members of the cat family, wolves and hyaenas were all hunted down and killed when they were known to be in the area. The situation for the Arabian leopard in some areas of Arabia is so critical that they are more in danger of extinction than the panda (which has become the symbol of threatened creatures). Some help for the Arabian leopard is at hand with the setting-up of protected areas where they can live without being persecuted, but laws saying they must not be hunted need to be enforced. Anyone who kills or captures the animals should be punished. Captive breeding programmes have been started, where a breeding centre in one country will exchange animals with a centre in another country. Records of the baby animals are kept with information about their parents, so a gene pool is built of healthy specimens. Fortunately, the organisations concerned about animals are working well together. This is a unique part of the world, as some of the creatures that live here are unknown anywhere else in the world. They are part of the heritage of the area and it is essential that they are not lost forever.

A rare Arabian wolf has few places to hide.

FACTOID

Sometimes wild cats breed with domestic cats. This pet's markings are just like the wild cat. True Gordon's wild cats are getting rarer and rarer because they are breeding with household pets.

Gordon's wild cat

Wild cats live in all continents of the world and three separate species are known to live in Arabia. Wild cats never become tame and live well away from humans, seeking shelter under bushes and tree roots. They catch wild prey, such as snakes, lizards, birds and small rodents. They spend much of their time in the branches of acacia trees.

Caracal

The Caracal lives either in the mountains or on the gravel plains, spending its day in its lair amongst the trees and bushes. It is very agile and can jump three metres high from a standing position. It is able to catch birds on the wing.

The Sand cat is the cat best adapted to the desert where it lives among the dunes. It must dig a den for its survival which may be more than a metre deep under the roots of the grass or bushes. The temperature in its den may be 10°C cooler than the outside air. It can survive without water for months at a time as it keeps still and cool in its den during the day. This helps it conserve moisture.

Sand cat

?

Are there still Arabian leopards in the wild?

The numbers of Arabian leopard have dropped so low that there may be fewer than two hundred of these beautiful animals left in the whole of the Arabian peninsula. They live in the most desolate and remote mountainous regions, mainly in Yemen, Saudi Arabia and Oman. They need caves to shelter from the sun and to hide from the people who hunt them.

After dragging their kill to a safe place, leopards return to feed on it later. They only eat a small amount of meat at one time, so they go back several times to the same kill. This habit increases their chances of being caught by hunters.

Breeding of Arabian leopard cubs in captivity is successfully producing healthy young cubs but cubs born in the wild still face many dangers from hunters and the destruction of their habitats.

Both leopards and wolves are hunted by trappers. Traps, made from large stones are about 120 cm long with a small entrance at one end. Bait, usually a goat, is fixed by rope to a large stone hung over the entrance. When the leopard takes the bait the stone falls down, trapping the animal inside.

Stone trap in the mountains.

Arabian leopard

ENDANGERED MAMMALS — IBEX AND ANTELOPES

Although efforts are being made to help mammals of Arabia survive as their habitats become eroded, the situation is still not a happy one. The antelope family breed well when they are in protected areas, but still suffer from poaching. Although the same variety of species still exist in Arabia as in the past, their numbers are greatly reduced. Some of them are even in danger of extinction. Herds of oryx, the largest of the antelopes living in Arabia, were the first to face this threat. They were hunted for food but, using traditional methods of hunting, stamina and patience were needed to catch them. Using four-wheel drive cars to follow the herds, and modern high-powered weapons to kill them needed no skills. Oryx became extinct in the wild. The last wild oryx were shot or removed in 1972. Fortunately, oryx caught in the area close to Oman's western border with Yemen were shipped to a zoo in the USA where they formed the basis of the 'World Herd'. Gradually they bred and oryx were re-introduced into Saudi Arabia and Oman to live in the wild, within protected areas. There are now also large oryx herds in the Gulf States in reserves and parks.

Horns of the ibex, embedded in the roof of a house in Yemen.

A herd of oryx

FACTOID

Arabian (or Mountain) gazelles are commonly seen in protected areas in all the countries of Arabia. Ten thousand of them form the largest herd, which roams freely in the Oryx Sanctuary in Oman.

Arabian gazelle

Rheem, or Sand gazelle

The Rheem, or Sand gazelle, is a shy animal that lives in family groups and travels great distances in search of new grazing. It is suffering from decreasing numbers and is now endangered.

Several hundred remaining ibex live in the mountainous regions of Arabia (*right*). The horns of the ibex can reach a full metre in length. Horns can be seen fixed to the roofs of houses in the Yemen (*left*), where they are thought to bring good luck.

Ibex

How were animals hunted in the past?

When the oryx was successfully hunted it provided a great deal of meat. All parts of the animal were used. Pouches and bags were made from its skin and the horn used to stiffen the central rib of women's masks. Meat was prepared by cutting it into strips and hanging it in a tree to dry. The Bedu had to trek for a day or two on their camels to find the oryx. The herd could move thirty or forty kilometres in a day. The only water the Bedu had with them was what they could carry in goat skins.

The Bedu used brushwood to make hiding places and then waited inside until the oryx came close. Sometimes they stalked the oryx by hiding behind a camel, walking in step with its back legs. They only emerged when they were close enough to take a shot at the oryx.

The Bedu's rifles had to be reloaded after only one shot. If the first shot missed, the herd scattered and a second shot was not possible. The herd had to be stalked again.

Saluki

Salukis were used in traditional hunting. Salukis are very fast dogs and can reach speeds of 60 km an hour.

REPTILES — SNAKES

Reptiles are the most efficiently adapted of all animals for desert survival. They can thrive in the most scorching sands where few other creatures can live. They do not get their body heat from the food they eat, but from the energy of the sun. If it is cold they have a low body temperature. When it is warm their temperature rises. Some reptiles increase their body heat by basking in the sun. Others are active at night lying on objects that the sun has warmed to get energy. They do not waste energy keeping their body temperature at a steady level but take on one that is close to their surroundings. If it is too hot or too cold reptiles become 'torpid', meaning slow and sleepy, which conserves energy. By using natural energy reptiles do not need to eat as frequently as birds or mammals of a similar size. Also, they need very little water to survive. Overlapping scales on reptiles' skin make the surface waterproof and they have no glands to release sweat. They have the lowest water loss rate from their bodies of all desert creatures.

?

Which snakes are harmless?

Many of the land snakes are harmless to humans or only mildly toxic. The fangs are fixed near the back of the upper jaw or they have many short teeth with no venom gland at all.

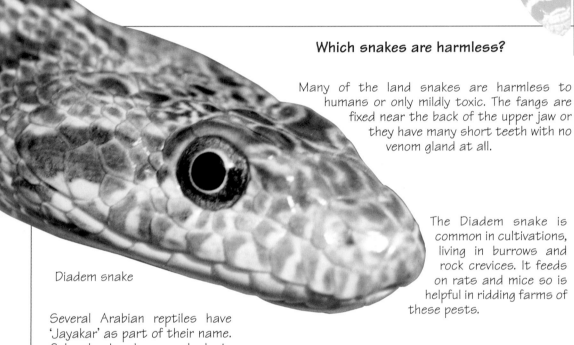

Diadem snake

The Diadem snake is common in cultivations, living in burrows and rock crevices. It feeds on rats and mice so is helpful in ridding farms of these pests.

Several Arabian reptiles have 'Jayakar' as part of their name. Colonel Jayakar worked in Muscat over a hundred years ago and sent specimens of creatures that he wanted to have identified back to Europe. When a person is the first to record a new species they have the honour of having that creature named after them. This still happens today as new species are discovered every year.

Jayakar's Sand Boa.

Colonel Jayakar inspecting the Sand Boa.

With small teeth and no venom to rely on, Boas use suffocation to catch their prey. Boas are particularly well adapted to living in the sand. Their scales are smooth and their eyes and nostrils are placed well up on their heads so that they can bury themselves and await their victims. This Jayakar's Sand Boa is squeezing a gecko tightly in its coils before devouring it.

Fear is often associated with snakes but they have fascinated humans since ancient times. Bronze and pottery snakes have been excavated by archaeologists from sites in Arabia and small metal snakes are attached to houses in Sana'a, Yemen. They are good luck symbols, thought to protect the house from evil.

Which snakes are venomous?

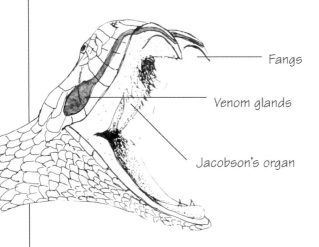

Fangs

Venom glands

Jacobson's organ

How is the venom injected?

All snakes eat live prey such as rodents, birds or other reptiles. Some species are equipped with fangs, which are used to strike their prey. The most dangerous snakes – vipers and asps – have long, hollow curved fangs. After the skin is pierced by the fangs, they act like hypodermic needles. Muscles compress the venom glands injecting the venom into its victim.

The nocturnal Horned viper is often found lying underneath a thin layer of sand so that only its eyes are visible. It lies silently waiting until a small animal comes close enough to get caught. **It is also dangerous to human beings and it is a good idea to wear shoes when walking on sand.**

Horned viper

Snakes have a very well developed sense of smell. They have a hollow pit in the roof of their mouths which acts as a sensory device. It is called the Jacobson's organ. Scents are picked up by its forked tongue and transferred to the roof of its mouth.

FACTOID

Sea snake

One drop of their venom from a Sea snake is enough to kill five men. Their poison is even stronger than that of their cousins, the cobras.

They are so well adapted to the sea that they can stay under the surface, without breathing, for as long as two hours. It can be even longer when they are resting.

There are about ten different species of sea snake identified in Arabian waters. The Yellow-bellied and the Arabian Gulf Sea snake are very widespread.

Sea snakes have flat tails shaped like paddles and give birth to live babies at sea.

REPTILES — LIZARDS

Reptiles have evolved very successfully to live in hot desert temperatures but they must take care not to overheat or, like all other creatures, they will die. Shade, sand, crevices or burrows are all places where lizards hide to avoid the heat. Skinks, chameleons and agamids are all members of the lizard family that are diurnal, which means active during the day, living on a diet of insects. Spiny-tailed lizards, also called *dhubs*, escape the heat by living in burrows, forming large colonies with as many as seventy active burrows. As night falls, the diurnal species are replaced by nocturnal lizards that forage for food while the ground is still warm from the sun. Geckos, one of the largest families of lizards, are mostly nocturnal.

?

Is a *Dhub* Lizard dangerous?

Although the *dhub* looks fierce, it is a gentle creature. When threatened, it puffs itself up with air to appear larger than it really is. Its tail can be used as a weapon to lash out at predators but it also escapes by dashing into its burrow. Since it is good to eat it has many enemies such as foxes, birds of prey and man, for whom roasted *dhub* is a delicacy.

The slate-grey *dhub* emerges from its burrow to warm itself in the sun. Gradually, its body turns a sulphury yellow as its blood heats up with only its head remaining grey. It has no need to drink water as it gets its moisture from its diet of plants.

What does it eat?

The *dhub* is an exception among the lizards in its eating habits, as the adults are totally vegetarian. Among the plants it lives on are:

Zygophyllum hamiense

One method of catching a *dhub* is to use a plank of wood through which nails have been banged. This has fine plastic threads attached to form nooses. The trap is placed at tne entrance to the burrow. As the *dhub* runs for cover, the nails hurt it and its leg is ensnared by the nooses. The plank is wedged across the entrance of the burrow. The hunter then uses the plank to pull the *dhub* out of the burrow. Sometimes it is so deep down in the hole it has to ɔe dug out.

Pennisetum divisum

Toad-headed agama

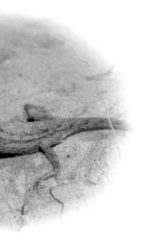

Big-headed gecko

Toad-headed agamas do not usually hunt actively but wait motionless for insects to pass close by. The male signals by waving and twirling its tail when it is agitated or wants to attract a mate.

Geckos are one of the largest families of lizards with more than 30 different species. Their large eyes, adapted for night vision, have vertical pupils like a cat's. Some species have toes with adhesive pads covered in tiny hooks, like Velcro, which enable them to run across vertical surfaces.

FACTOID

Sand skink

Sand skinks, have the appearance of both lizards and snakes. Their bodies are long and thin with very tiny legs.

They have a wedge-shaped snout and smooth scales which enable them to dive under the sand when threatened.

Chameleon

A chameleon's eyes move in all directions, each eye working on its own so it has two different views of its surroundings. The pictures are co-ordinated by its brain.

Chameleons only live in the moist area of Arabia. They are perfectly fashioned for clasping and moving through trees and bushes.

The eyelids are fused together with a small hole in the centre acting as the pupil. It has binocular vision so it can judge distances very accurately when catching its victim.

The tail is prehensile (capable of grasping), acting like another hand to grip tightly or to balance the weight of the chameleon as it moves cautiously through the trees.

Its prehensile tongue is as long as the chameleon itself. When resting, its tongue is rolled back in a spiral on the floor of its mouth. A chameleon 30 cm long can catch an insect 26 cm away.

A chameleon has two bunches of toes. One bunch has three toes and the other two toes. The bunches oppose each other, so it can grip with precision.

MIGRATION

Some birds are adapted to cope with extreme temperatures such as the summer heat of the desert. They stay in Arabia all year round. They are known as residents. Other birds take advantage of the cool winter weather to visit for a few months, or they pass through Arabia on their way to other countries. In the autumn and spring, a vast number of different species can be seen passing through Arabia. Not only birds migrate. Many different creatures go in search of a better source of food, from small butterflies to huge whales. Turtles return to the beach where they were born to breed every few years, but for the rest of their lives they swim thousands of kilometres foraging for food. Scientists are trying to collect more information about where different creatures go when they migrate. Turtles have been tagged and birds ringed so they can be followed during their lifetime. Although some questions can be answered by these methods, migration still remains one of the great mysteries of the animal kingdom.

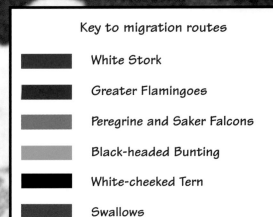

Many butterflies only visit Arabia in the winter months when flowering plants are plentiful.

The Brown Veined and the Painted Lady butterflies migrate in spectacular numbers from October to May. Some butterflies have a local migration, just moving a few kilometres to where there are more plants.

Key to migration routes

	White Stork
	Greater Flamingoes
	Peregrine and Saker Falcons
	Black-headed Bunting
	White-cheeked Tern
	Swallows

Black-headed Bunting

The Bedu make a winter migration with their camels in search of fresh grazing. They follow the rains knowing that plenty of plants will soon sprout green shoots.

Some tribes have to migrate for long distances. Others find fresh grazing nearby and may only travel for fifteen or twenty kilometres. In summertime, they have to settle near to a water source. They stay there all through the hot weather until the rains come again in the winter. However, not many Bedu now follow this traditional way of life. Some still live in tents but most are now settled in one place.

There is a general movement of birds southwards in autumn and another northwards each spring.

The location of Arabia on a migratory crossroads makes for interesting bird watching. Every autumn probably some two to three thousand million birds move southwards through Arabia to winter in eastern and southern Africa. Each species has its own route. Most birds avoid crossing the sea and stay close to the coastline.

White Stork

There is a massive migration of shorebirds from Central Asia and Siberia into Arabia and on to Africa. Gulls, terns, plovers, dunlin and curlews are among the many species to be seen on the shores in the winter months.

White-cheeked Tern

The routes taken by swallows are very broad and may also be taken by most land birds, including falcons.

Swallows

Peregrine and Saker falcons

The falcons are trapped on the coastline as they arrive.

!

FACTOID

Humpback whales travel from warm seas to the polar regions, and back again, every year. The winter months are spent in the warmth, giving birth to young and the summer months in the cold oceans where there are large amounts of fish. However, it has been noticed that the Humpback whales living in Oman's waters do not migrate as food is always plentiful. Are they different from other Humpback whales? At present it is still a mystery.

Fish are known to migrate in the summer months from the hot, salty waters of the Arabian Gulf into the cooler seas of the Gulf of Oman and the Indian Ocean, where an 'up-welling' of plankton rich water is very nutritious.

Greater Flamingoes

POLAR REGIONS

BIRDS OF THE DESERT

For much of the year the vegetation of the desert is shrivelled and brown. Birds of prey circle overhead in the blue sky and meat-eating mammals and reptiles search for food among the plants. Yet ground-dwelling desert birds choose this hostile environment to live and breed. They have several adaptations to help them survive. Most desert birds are pale, sandy coloured. Pale colours reduce the amount of heat that is absorbed. Most seek shade during the day. Grey or brown markings on their feathers camouflage them from predators. Hidden under low shrubby bushes, they only emerge in the early morning or evening to feed. Large eyes enable them to spot insects in the fading light. During years of drought almost no rain falls at all. Both plant life and insects are reduced in quantity and quality. The population of desert birds suffers. In extremely arid areas, such as the Rub al Khali (the Empty Quarter), there is almost no bird life at all.

A Spotted Thick-knee (left) and a Houbara Bustard chick, (right) sheltering under bushes in the desert, show how effective camouflage can be. If a predator comes too close to her nest, the mother bird leads it away by pretending to be injured. Her wings drag on the ground so the predator follows her thinking she is an easy target. When she is far away from the nest she flies off.

Desert birds must protect their eggs from direct sunlight. Even a few minutes exposed to the sun's powerful rays will cause chicks inside the eggs to die. Many birds stand over the eggs rather than sitting on them. This keeps them shaded and ventilated. Nests are made in a scrape in the ground, under the shade of a rock or bush.

Desert birds are able to cool themselves by panting. With its beak open, the bird raises and lowers the floor of its mouth very fast. This passes air over the moist parts of its mouth. As the moisture evaporates, the bird is cooled.

Insects are very important to the eco-system of the desert. The diet of desert birds is almost 100 per cent insects. Insect-eating birds do not need much additional water, as insects have liquid nourishment in them.

Grey Francolin

Crested Skylark

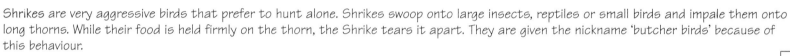

Great Grey Shrike

Shrikes are very aggressive birds that prefer to hunt alone. Shrikes swoop onto large insects, reptiles or small birds and impale them onto long thorns. While their food is held firmly on the thorn, the Shrike tears it apart. They are given the nickname 'butcher birds' because of this behaviour.

What do shrikes like to eat?

Although the Great Grey Shrike is only about 24 cm long, it is prepared to attack creatures almost as large as itself. One bird was seen to kill a lizard 15 cm long by digging into its throat.

A shrike was photographed attacking a poisonous viper so large that it couldn't pick it up. It cut the viper into two pieces with its beak, flying off with one piece at a time.

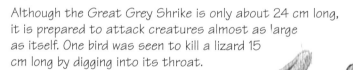

Chestnut-bellied sandgrouse
The sandgrouse is the exception amongst desert birds in that it needs a regular supply of water to survive. It is a model of how birds can adapt to live in a difficult environment.

Sandgrouse live on a diet of seeds which lack moisture. Every morning and evening they may fly as far as 60 kilometres to the nearest source of fresh water to drink.

FACTOID

The feathers of a sandgrouse can contain more water than a kitchen sponge.

Their chicks are not able to fly to water so the adult male carries it to them. He soaks the feathers on his abdomen with water. Back at the nest the chicks strip the water from his feathers.

BIRDS — IN THE TOWNS

In the past, many varieties of birds that were resident in countries near the Arabian peninsula were not able to survive in desert environments, as suitable food was not available for them. However, the greening of the desert that has taken place in all the large cities and towns has changed the situation for many species. Avenues of trees along the highways, parks filled with flowers and grasses, lakes and gardens have all encouraged birds with a wide range of food needs to make the Arabian peninsula their home. Both plants and water attract insects. Flowers provide nectar and seeds. Birds are quick to move in and take over habitats that suit their needs. They have wasted no time in settling into their new homes and some stay all year round. They have now joined the residents that were already adapted to the desert habitats and become residents themselves.

The Purple Sunbird builds an unusual hanging nest which has a side entrance.

The male Purple Sunbird has glistening plumage during the breeding season. The female is a drab brown with yellow underparts. As they hover by nectar-giving flowers, they look just like hummingbirds. As well as sucking nectar from garden flowers, such as hibiscus, they also seek out the desert plant, Sodom's apple, which is avoided by most other birds.

What are Hoopoes looking for?

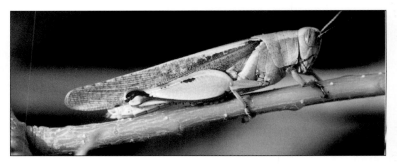

Crickets and grasshoppers are vegetarian insects that generally feed on grass. They lay their eggs under the ground.

The Hoopoe is a bird everyone quickly notices. It has unusual colouring and a long curved beak. The crest of feathers on its head is raised when it is alarmed or excited.

Hoopoes spend a great deal of time on the ground, working their way backwards and forwards across the grass. Several of these birds often appear together jabbing at the ground with their long beaks. Then they scurry across to the next piece of grass to be cleared of insects.

The species called Mole crickets are the favourite diet of the Hoopoes. The front legs of the mole cricket are very powerful and fitted with little claws. It spends much of its life underground and excavates tunnels where it lives on a diet of roots and small insects. The female Mole cricket lays her eggs in underground chambers which she guards.

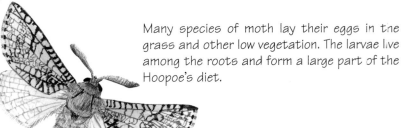

Many species of moth lay their eggs in the grass and other low vegetation. The larvae live among the roots and form a large part of the Hoopoe's diet.

The Escapees
The birds known as escapees are those which were probably brought to the area by bird dealers. Having either escaped from captivity or been set free by people who could no longer care for them, these birds have set up home in the wild and become successful at looking after themselves.

KEY TO GARDEN BIRDS CHART

1. Common Mynahs
Common Mynahs strutt across the grass, noisily arguing with each other. Mynah birds can mimic the sounds made by other birds and sometimes human voices. This is probably why they were thought to make good pets.

2. The Ring-necked Parakeet
These parakeets have bred so successfully that they are now regarded as pests and are not allowed to be imported into the Arabian peninsula. They like to feast on ripening dates, which does not make them popular with the farmers.

3. Bulbuls
Several varieties of Bulbuls live in the parks and gardens. Often seen in groups, there are Red-vented Bulbuls, with red feathers underneath their tails and Yellow-vented Bulbuls with yellow underparts. The White-cheeked Bulbuls are noticeable by their white face feathers. They nest in the bushes and the trees.

5. The Graceful Warbler is a small bird with pale brown plumage. It flicks its tail all the time it is darting amongst fallen leaves searching for insects.

4. House Sparrows
Flocks of house sparrows peck busily around the seedheads of grasses. They are sociable birds and never appear by themselves. They are very adaptable and live in many areas around the world.

Birds feed on a wide variety of foods, such as fruits, seeds, nectar and insects. Their beaks are adapted so they can easily deal wth their chosen diet.

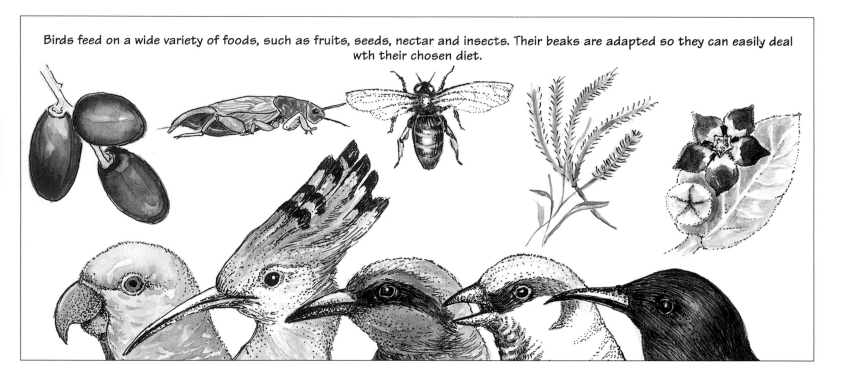

BIRDS — IN NEW CULTIVATIONS

The number of people living in the Arabian peninsula has increased enormously since the discovery of oil. For some birds man's activities threaten their habitats, but for others it increases the number of places where they can thrive. There is a need to grow more food for all the extra people so farmers are growing crops, fruit and vegetables. Forests of trees that grow well in the desert, such as *ghaf,* mesquite and acacia trees, have also been newly planted. People like to relax after work so facilities for sports have been provided. Big green expanses of grass have sprung up across the peninsula with artificial lakes. Cool sheltered refuges from the desert heat continue to appear and so do the numbers of birds that enjoy them.

The brilliant blue feathers of the **Indian Roller** cannot be missed. It gets it name from its rolling, dipping flight. It often sits on a prominent perch, such as poles, wires or dead trees.

Bee-eaters

Bee-eaters can often be seen in open country, perching on the trees or wires. The most common are the Little Green Bee-eater and the Blue-cheeked Bee-eater.

The Little Green Bee-eater

Blue-cheeked Bee-eater

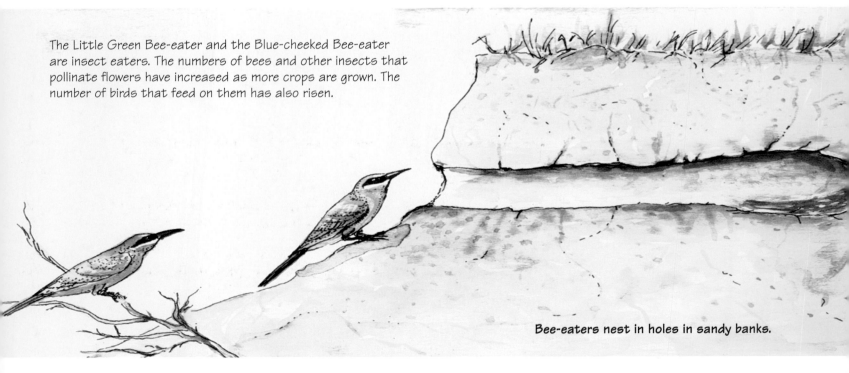

The Little Green Bee-eater and the Blue-cheeked Bee-eater are insect eaters. The numbers of bees and other insects that pollinate flowers have increased as more crops are grown. The number of birds that feed on them has also risen.

Bee-eaters nest in holes in sandy banks.

Water birds feed on many different types of food. They find plenty to in eat both fresh and salt water wetlands that have been created in the region.

Curlew

Duck

Heron

Flamingo

The Grey Heron
There are many species of heron in Arabia, from the huge Goliath heron to small egrets. Herons are often seen standing like statues in the water looking for a meal to pass by. Their long pointed beaks stab their prey.

Curlews with their long curved bills probe the mud for small creatures to eat. They are winter visitors, although some non-breeding birds stay over the summer months. They are happy in both fresh water pools and shallow salt lagoons.

Ducks
The largest and most well known of the duck family is the mallard. The male has a gleaming green head in the breeding season. The rest of the year he is nearer in colour to the brown female. Mallards can be seen in almost any wetland from wadis to sea-coasts and lagoons.

Greater Flamingoes
live on salt-water lagoons 'puddling' in the water. They bend their legs at the knee and push their feet into the mud stirring up tiny shrimps. Lowering their heads into the water they dredge the upper part of their beaks through the mud. A fringe of fine slits act like a sieve. The lower half of their beaks move up and down pumping water out of their mouths, leaving the food behind.

FACTOID

Sometimes birds that seem to be brightly painted appear among the flocks of Indian Silverbills. They have been dyed by the owners of pet shops to make them look more attractive. The dye disappears after a few weeks, and they become brownish again.

BIRDS OF PREY

In winter time the sky over the Arabian Peninsula is filled with birds of prey, known as raptors. Vultures, falcons, hawks and eagles all pass through on their migration routes, or spend winter in the warm climate. Some of the species breed in the region. Vultures are scavengers, clearing up dead carcasses, but most birds of prey are specially adapted to hunt live food during daylight hours. They need to be stronger, faster and sharper than the creature they catch. They are phenomenal acrobats in the air as they twist, turn and dive in pursuit of their prey. Owls are also birds of prey that hunt during the night. They are adapted to glide silently through the darkness, their large eyes seeking out any movement on the the ground below.

Griffon vultures live in south-west Arabia. Their wing span can be 2.5 metres across. They search over huge distances for dead meat, known as carrion. The meat is held down by their feet and bite-sized pieces are torn off with their beaks.

The flying skills of birds of prey are in a world class of their own. They fly at altitudes at which human beings would need supplementary oxygen. Mammals have lungs that act like bellows that inflate and deflate but birds constantly extract oxygen from the air as it passes through their lungs.

Flying takes up a great deal of strength and energy. The diet of birds of prey is very nourishing and high in energy. The Kestrel (*left*) hovers above the ground barely moving its wings as it looks for grass-hoppers and large beetles in the desert and grasses below.

The Bonelli's Eagle (*right*) is a small eagle that occasionally breeds in Arabia. It is an endangered species. It is a booted eagle, which is a name given to eagles with feathers extending down their legs.

The male has a spectacular flight display when it is trying to attract a mate. He plunges from a great height, with folded wings. Then he climbs, drops and makes a long fast dash at a low level towards the foot of the cliff chosen for the nest site.

The beak of a vulture (*above*) is shaped for tearing flesh.

Why is the Osprey nicknamed 'the fish hawk'?

The untidy stick nests of the Osprey can be seen all around the coast line of the Arabian peninsula. Breeding sites are sometimes near cities and the birds do not seem to be disturbed by noise.

The Osprey is sometimes nicknamed the fish hawk because its diet consists solely of fish.

The Osprey searches for a fish in the water below.

The dive or 'stoop'

1. As it dives, its wings are swept back against its body. Its tail closes like a fan and steers the body towards its prey.

2. As it approaches the water its feet go forward, talons outstretched to catch the fish. The flight feathers at the tips of the wings spread out to lessen the drag of air across them.

3. Its feet, not its beak, are the most formidable weapons of a bird of prey. The Osprey has sharp scales between the toes to hold onto its slippery prey.

4. The Osprey takes off with the fish gripped firmly by its feet.

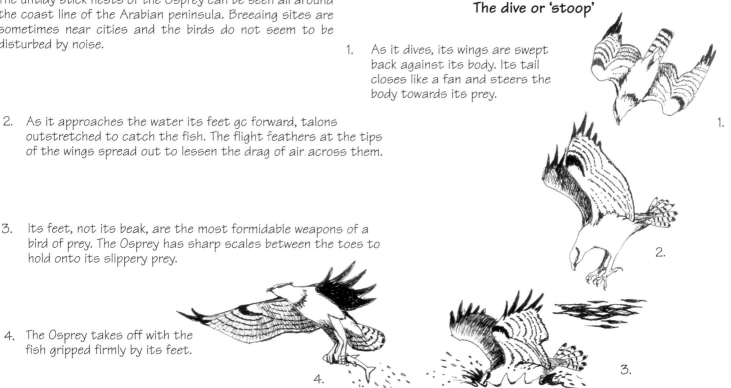

Several varieties of owl live and breed in Arabia, like the Desert Eagle Owl (below) Their feathers are soft with fuzzy edges to muffle the sounds of their flight at night. Their prey is generally swallowed whole, so their beaks do not have a hook on the end for tearing up flesh.

FACTOID

The eyeballs of birds of prey are very large in relation to the size of their heads. Falcons' eyes occupy fifteen times more space within their head than the space that is taken up by human eyes.

Also, their eyes are placed in their head in a forward-looking position, so the image they receive of their prey overlaps. This helps them pinpoint accurately where it is.

BIRDS OF THE SEA AND SHORE

The long coast of the Arabian peninsula attracts sea birds in huge numbers. Off-shore islands, lagoons, sandy shores and stony beaches are among the many habitats available to birds. The sea teems with marine life and vast numbers of creatures live on the seashore, providing a rich diet for seabirds. Many species of seabirds are migratory but others live and breed in the area. A few species are only found in this part of the world and nowhere else. They are called endemic. As the human population grows, man's activities are disturbing some of the seashore habitats. Cats have been taken to places where sea birds breed to control rodents, but have found the nesting birds much easier prey. Colonies of nesting birds get protection in some areas but more sites are needed where they can breed in safety.

Gulls prey upon babies of cormorants. Their long beaks, ending with a hook, enable gulls to pull apart their food. Cormorant eggs are also a delicacy for the villagers who live near breeding sites.

Cormorants are attracted to shoals of fish and settle on the water above the shoal. They have two fishing methods. One is to dive down from a sitting position on the surface of the water, and the other is to plunge – dive from the air.

Unlike other water birds, their feathers do not trap air which enables them to dive swiftly and overtake their prey.

FACTOID

!

Some species are given special protection to enable them to breed in peace. This sign tells people that the Crab Plover colony must be respected. People who ignore this sign will be punished.

The Crab Plover is a wading bird that migrates to the Arabian peninsula and breeds in several locations. Crab Plovers live in colonies, many birds living and breeding in the same area. They are the only waders in the world which make their nests in holes in the ground.

Socotra Cormorants breed on the southern coast of the Arabian peninsula. Their nests are just circular scrapes in the ground. Cormorants are clumsy parents and the eggs are often trodden on or knocked out of the nest.

Crab Plovers excavate nest burrows more than two metres long and half a metre deep in sandy banks. Only one egg is laid. It is white. There is no need for the egg to be camouflaged as it is laid underground. Maybe the egg is white so it can be easily spotted by the Crab Plover in the darkness. Crab Plovers rely upon crabs for their diet and eat very little else.

The Socotra Cormorant is considered a threatened species and international efforts are being made to study them and their needs.

How can you tell if a bird is a seagull or a tern?

Two major families of seabirds are gulls and terns. There are many different species, but gulls are generally larger than terns.

Look out for the body shapes to tell you whether a bird is a gull or tern.

Gulls: Heavy bodies and thick beaks. Often scavenge for food on the beach.

Terns: Long, pointed wings Slender, sharp beaks. Plunge into sea after fish.

A colony of Lesser Crested Terns nesting on the beach.

Nests of seabirds are often just scrapes in the soil. Eggs are spotted, to camouflage them from predators.

A group of birds, known as waders, also live on the shore and by the lagoons. Waders have long, thin legs. As they search for food at the water's edge their feet, with long spread out toes, distribute their weight evenly across the sand or mud. This stops them from sinking into the soft seashore.

Black winged stilt

Terek sandpiper

The Common Snipe and Terek Sandpiper are two wading birds with very different beaks. There is a huge variety of beaks and legs to be seen on the shore. No opportunity to probe, stab or sieve for food is lost. Every bird has its own special adaptions to choose a menu from the creatures living there.

Common snipe

PLANTS IN THE DESERT

In the deserts and mountains of Arabia, plants, like animals, must adapt in order to survive harsh conditions. Soil, water, wind and temperature all affect plants that grow there. Animals and man are also hazards that plants have to overcome in their struggle to survive. Grazing herds of goats and camels destroy them. Man reduces the level of underground water by pumping it out for his own needs. Plants can be divided into two main types. There are perennials which can be woody or succulent and are seen all year round. The second type are annuals that only appear in cool winter months. The perennials are soldier plants. They are tough plants that can cope with the heat, wind and lack of rain. Their foliage dies back in the summer and they may appear dead but their roots are alive beneath the ground. Annuals opt out of the intense heat of summer by remaining dormant, or sleeping, as seeds in the ground.

Juniper berries are used to flavour food.

?

Which plants are in the group called woody perennials?

Woody perennials include most of the trees and large shrubs. The **Ghaf tree** is one of the most common trees in sandy desert areas but it also thrives on rocky plains and in wadi beds. Roots of Ghaf trees have been known to go down 60 metres below ground.

Ghaf tree (Prosopis cineraria)

One common large bush is **Calatropis Procera**, known as **Sodom's apple**. It is a milkweed, which secretes a milky juice or latex whenever a leaf or stem is broken off.

Acacias are widespread on gravel plains and in the foothills of mountains. Their central root systems are able to tap into deep aquifers, reservoirs of water below ground. They are slow growing and their seeds are very tough. The lower branches are heavily grazed by camels and goats. Desert trees do not like to be crowded together. They are spaced out because there is not enough water to share.

Acacia tree (Acacia tortilis)

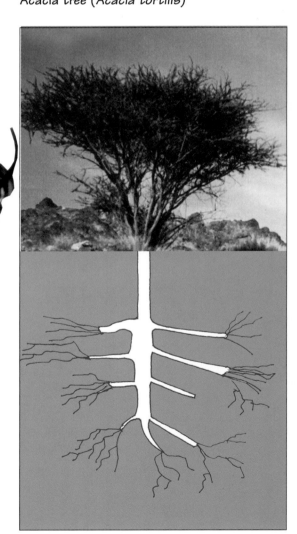

All parts of the Sodom's apple are poisonous so it is not eaten by animals. However, it is the favourite food of **Plain Tiger** caterpillars. Bitter latex in the plant makes the caterpillars taste bad to their predators.

Some varieties of trees are specially well-suited to mountainous conditions. Junipers are the dominant tree in the mountains of south-west Saudi Arabia, Yemen and parts of Oman.

The trees can reach 15-20 metres high.

Perennial trees provide homes and food for many birds and insects.

Yellow-vented Bulbul

These mountain forests of juniper trees are very important places for birds, some of which only live in these high wooded areas.

Yemen Linnets feed on juniper berries.

?

Which plants in the group are called succulent perennials (Halophytes)?

Soil near the coast and in dips in the desert is very saline, or salty, where ancient lakebeds once lay. These areas are known as sabkha. The soil is poor in nutrients. A common plant along the coastline of the Arabian Gulf is *Zygophyllum hamiense* which has swollen round leaves.

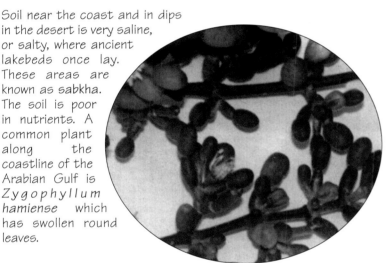

!

FACTOID

The Desert Hyacinth or Basal (*Cistanche tubulosa*)

Some plants have cleverly devised a method of getting energy without working for it. The Desert Hyacinth has no green leaves to make its food from the sun's light so it attaches itself to the roots of other plants and draws its nourishment from that source instead.

?

How do flowers manage to survive in the desert when there is no water?

Plants known as annuals are only visible for a short part of the year. Their seeds lie sleeping in the soil and only germinate after heavy rain. They do not germinate after a short shower, as the moisture is not sufficient to soften their seedcase. In very dry years no annuals flower at all. When rain falls, annuals respond very quickly to it. They are able to produce flowers, fruits and seeds in only two months. Then the seeds lie sleeping, once again, waiting for another rainy spell before they germinate. Sometimes their wait will last as long as thirty years.

Pink Mustard (*Erucaria hispanica*)

Blue pimpernel (*Anagallis arvensis*)

Arabian primrose (*Arnebria histidissima*)

PLANTS – HOW THEY ADAPT

As rainfall is very light and infrequent, it is essential for plants to prevent loss of moisture. One way of conserving water is to reduce the area of the leaves. Most desert plants have very small leaves and in some plants leaves are almost absent. Direct sunlight is kept away from plants by hairs, thorns and prickles which also prevent them being eaten by animals. Trees play a very important part in the life of both people and wild creatures. They provide food, shade and protection. Their wood and leaves were essential building materials in the past and were also used as fuel for fires.

Acacia twigs have small leaves arranged either side of a central stem. Their long thorns and woody stalks show how plants have evolved to discourage animals from eating them. Their many white or yellow flowers are rich in nectar sought after by honey bees.

Plants known as succulents store water in their fat leaves. The surface of the leaf is waxy, cutting down water loss. The outer leaves or stem cells can swell increasing their volume, so more water can be stored.

Red thumb (Cynomorium coccineum) has no green parts. It is a parasite, growing off the roots of another plant. It gets all its energy from the host plant.

In plants where leaves are almost absent, photosynthesis, a chemical process which converts the sun's energy into food, is carried out by the green stem and branches. Flowers on desert plants are also small. Arta has delicate pink flowers but its red, furry fruits are more eyecatching. They were used to make a painting material in the past.

Arta (Calligonum comosum)

Acacia also known as simr (Acacia tortilis).

Some plants have leaves with a furry surface of fine, or white, hairs. These reflect the harsh rays of the sun and create a humid microclimate around the plant. Hairs also break up the surface of the leaf so there is less chance of water loss.

Beware – Poisonous!

All parts of the **Oleander**, frequently seen growing wild in the wadis are poisonous. This is their defence mechanism against animals and prevents them from being eaten.

Oleander or Haban.
(Nerium mascatense)

How did people use the plants of Arabia to make medicines?

In the past, people used many desert plants in their daily lives. One of the most important uses was for healing. Hundreds of different plants were used to make herbal remedies. Many people still consider them to be the best form of medicine today. The skills of making herbal medicines are passed from one generation to the next.

Arak Rak is a shrubby plant often called the Arabian toothbrush. Branches or roots are cut up into sticks about 15 cm long. They are sun-dried and sold to the shops in small bundles. Before using the stick as a toothbrush, the bark is removed and the end of the stick is soaked and chewed. The wood has a medicinal flavour.

Arakh Rak or Toothbrush tree (Salvadora persica)

Arabian toothbrush

Sidr tree
(Ziziphus spina-christi)

The fruits of the sidr are sold at market stalls and are good to eat.

Many different parts of the sidr tree are used for medicines. The seeds are powdered with lemon juice and used to treat liver complaints. Roots are used for painful conditions such as arthritis and rheumatism. The fruits are used for bronchitis and coughs. It is an important food source for insects, birds, animals and people.

Blepharis ciliaris is known as the Eyelash plant (left).

It grows in the mountains and high gravel plains. Vicious thorns protect it from animals. Wood ash from roots of the plants was used to make kohl. Kohl was applied to the rims of eyes to protect them from disease. Antimony, a brittle lustrous metal, was also used to make kohl.

A veiled lady with kohl around her eyes.

MANGROVES AND LAGOONS

A mangrove forest is different from any other kind of forest on earth. The mangrove trees survive in salty, inter-tidal, shallow lagoons where few other plants can grow. The muddy soil of the lagoons contains almost no oxygen, an essential requirement for most plant life. In the roots of the mangrove, a wealth of animal life thrives and breeds. The mangrove forests are important nurseries for molluscs and many species of fish that are sold in the souqs. They breed among the mangroves where they are protected by the root systems of the trees. Fish have always been the main diet of people living on the coast, so it is important that the mangrove forests remain healthy habitats for the fish to breed. Large numbers of migratory birds rest or stay over winter. Today, many of these water habitats are protected areas so that the birds are not disturbed.

Blue crabs with long spiny pincers provide nourishment for many birds.

The vertical roots of the mangrove tree are air-breathing. The roots do an important job preventing soil of the lagoons being eroded by the sea.

Fiddler crabs have one small and one huge claw which they move up and down sifting through the mud and debris underneath the trees. Their eyes are on stalks.

Underneath the trees, live creatures that use the roots for protection. An eco-system of birds, crabs, fish, snails and shellfish live in the lagoon, all dependent on each other for food.

Tree snails (right) climb among the leaves of the mangroves.

(Below) Terebralia, a type of shellfish living in the mud.

The green and fleshy seeds of the trees drop down into the mud when they are about 3 cm long. The roots, looking like an upside-down umbrella, grow to support a new tree.

The White-collared kingfisher (right) is an endemic species. They make their nests in holes in the trunks and branches of old mangroves at Khor Kalba in the United Arab Emirates and Jeddah, Saudi Arabia.

A mangrove forest

?

Why are the lagoons of Arabia home to huge flocks of flamingoes?

Greater Flamingo breeding grounds are in Iran. They build mud nests and show signs of breeding activity when wintering in Arabia, but few of their attempts are successful. The nests are sometimes washed away by the tides and they are easily disturbed by man's activities.

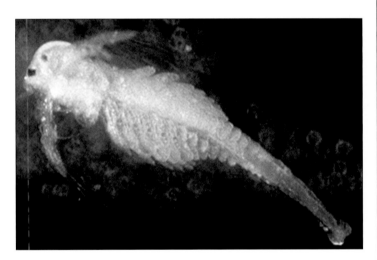

The parents take turns sitting on the egg to keep it warm. If sucessful, the egg will hatch after thirty days. Flamingoes can fly 400 kilometres in one night to find food for their young. They may live for forty years.

Artemia or brine shrimp are the preferred diet of the Greater Flamingo. The flamingoes in Arabia can be white or pink. It is not usual for them to breed here. Pink feathers are their breeding plumage.

!

FACTOID

Many flamingoes are ringed with a *darvik ring* (below). Details on these darvik rings, which are attached to the flamingoe's leg, identify where it was born. The information on the rings can be read from 100 metres away with binoculars. Useful data is collected about the movement of the birds as they migrate to different breeding sites.

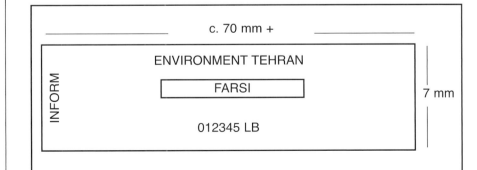

c. 70 mm +

INFORM

ENVIRONMENT TEHRAN

FARSI

7 mm

012345 LB

FOSSILS — ANCIENT LIFE ON EARTH

Fossils are the remains of plants and animals that lived long ago, preserved in rock. It is usually only the hard parts of animals and plants such as bones, shells, teeth or woody parts of trees that are able to survive the process of fossilisation. Soft parts quickly decompose. Sea creatures are the main types of fossil found in the rocks of the Arabian peninsula. As the earth was formed, the continents changed positions. The climate altered many times and Arabia was covered by sea. Although we do not notice it, the surface of the earth is still constantly moving. Over millions of years, the surface rocks are buried and folded deep in the earth. They can also be lifted up again and eroded to expose the fossils. By studying these, we can see a selection of life that existed in a time so ancient that it is known as pre-history.

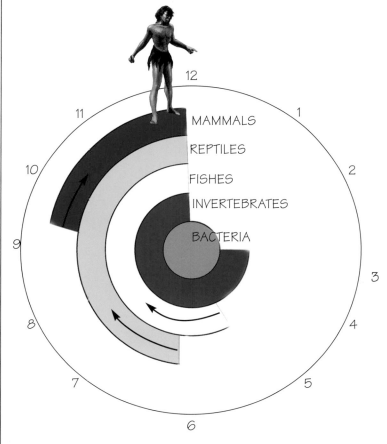

Fossils show that Arabia was a corridor where animals passed between Africa and Asia. The fossilised jaw of a hippopotamus (*above*) and also teeth of elephants that lived 35 to 15 million years ago have been found.

How were fossils formed in Arabia? **?**

1. When a creature or plant dies it must be buried quickly by sand or mud in order to fossilise. It remains under the sand which gradually turns to sedimentary rock as more and more layers press down on it. The fossils are trapped in the rock.

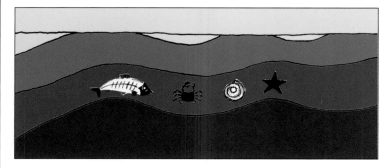

2. As the earth's crust slowly moves, the layers of rock on the surface are eroded by water and weather.

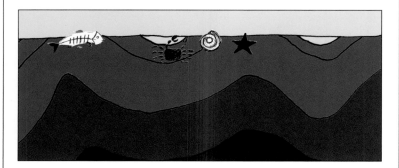

3. Some fossils become exposed for people to find. Shelled animals are the most common fossils found in the Arabian peninsula.

The geological clock

The earth formed 4,600,000,000 (4.6 billion) years ago but it is only in the last 600 million years that recognisable fossils became common.

MAMMALS
REPTILES
FISHES
INVERTEBRATES
BACTERIA

This circle represents the last 600 million years, which is only about one-tenth of the earth's history. It shows when different creatures appeared on earth.

Each hour on the clock represents 50 million years.

Man appeared less than a minute before midnight.

FACTOID

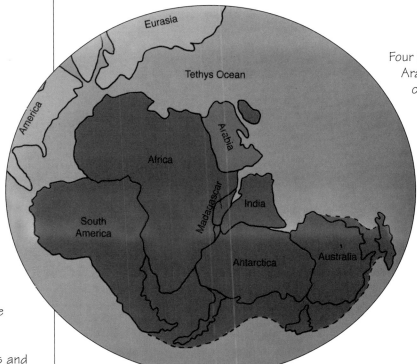

Four hundred million years ago, Arabia and all the southern continents formed one huge continent called Gondwanaland.

The same marine animals could be found from Arabia to Europe. They lived in a vast ocean called Tethys, that has long since closed over.

The mountain range along the eastern edge of the Arabian peninsula shows clearly the layering of sedimentary rocks and how they have been tilted by the movement of the earth's crust. These mountains are a good place to search for fossils.

Gastropod fossils with snail-like shells are frequently found.

Geologists from the oil industry use fossils as one method for dating the age of oil-bearing sediments.

What do fossils in the sea reveal?

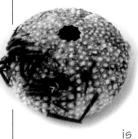

These creatures are close relatives in the family called echinoids. Starfish are in the same family. When a sea urchin (*above*) is alive it has long spines but these are lost during fossilisation and only the skeleton remains. These are known as 'tests' which are made up of five plates that lock together.

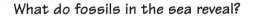

Sand dollars are flattened sea urchins with a central hole underneath through which they feed. The flower-like pattern on the top has five symmetrical petals.

Corals
The hard chalky skeleton of coral polyps formed fossil rock, which was used as a building material in the coastal towns of Arabia.

SEALIFE — SEASHELLS

Seashells are homes made and lived in by creatures called molluscs, which means 'soft-bodied'. Molluscs are invertebrates, creatures with no backbones, so the shell protects their body. Some molluscs like rocky shores, others like sandy beaches. When the mollusc dies, the shell is left empty, and there is great pleasure to be had collecting shells washed up onto the beach. The beauty of shells lies in the huge variety of forms they take. Some are so tiny that they are hardly noticeable on the sand. Others are large and eye-catching. The mantle of the slug-like creatures living inside the shell produces the detailed patterns and exquisite colours of each species. Every time the tide washes across the beach, a new treasure trove of shells is left behind.

A shell moving fast across the beach has been taken over by a Hermit crab. The body of a Hermit Crab is soft and vulnerable to predators. It moves into a new shell each time its body grows too large for the old one.

?

What are the two main types of sea creatures known as molluscs?

Gastropods

Most gastropods have an operculum, a trap door that seals the shell tight when the body is pulled inside. Some gastropods have other ways of ensuring their safety and don't have an operculum.

Siphon

operculum

A large flat muscular foot is used to creep about on. It secretes a **mucus** which gives the gastropod a base to slide on across sand and rocks.

The **radula**, equipped with teeth.

Bivalves

Bivalves have hinged shells kept open by a ligament. The two halves are closed by strong muscles. The shell of a bivalve grows from the beak. Their diet is of microscopic sea creatures suspended in the water.

The beak

Siphons

Both gastropods and bivalves inhale water through a siphon. Waste products and water are exhaled through a second siphon.

Some of the gastropods found on Arabian beaches:

1. Spiny Murex, 2. Augur shell, 3. Turret shell, 4/5 Cowries, 6 Immature Cowrie, 7. Sundial shells, 8. *Umbonium vestiarium*

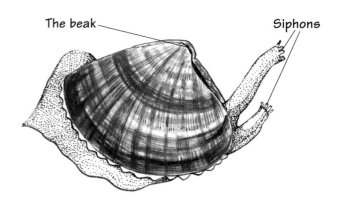

1.

4.

5.

3.

6.

7.

8.

One part of the mollusc's body is unique to these creatures. It is a fold of membrane called a mantle. The calcium shell of the creature is made by the mantle. When the mantle is fully extended it almost covers the shell. It can be pulled into the cavity between the body of the animal and its shell. Then the surface of the shell is exposed.

Some gastropods are carnivorous and highly aggressive towards other molluscs. The Moon snail traps bivalves and other gastropods with its huge fleshy foot. It drills a hole in the shell of its victim with teeth on its radula. The Moon Snail sucks the soft body of the creature inside through the hole it has made.

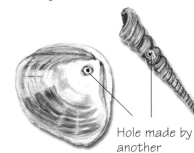

Hole made by another gastropod.

A Paper nautilus (*left*) is not a shell, but the egg-case of an octopus. The octopus secretes the shell-like material from which the nautilus is formed and carries it around until the eggs hatch.

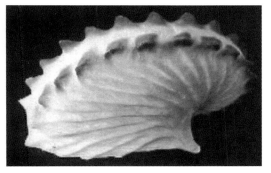

Can a shell be dangerous?

Beware of cone shells. Those with tent-like markings are particularly poisonous. The animal that inhabits a cone shell has a poisonous dart in its proboscis, which extends from the end of the shell. The venom from the dart can produce serious reactions and even death in some people.

Some of the bivalves found on Arabian beaches:

1. Pearl Oyster, 2. Scallop, 3&4, Thorny oysters, 5. Razor shell, 6. Cockle

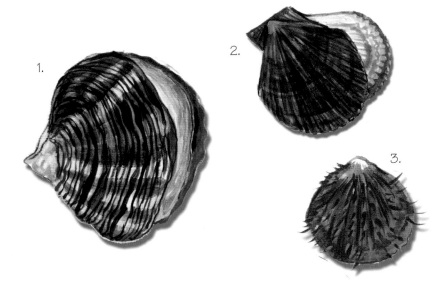

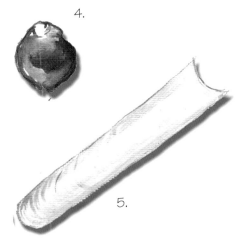

1.

2.

3.

4.

5.

6.

SEALIFE — TURTLES

The long eastern coastline of the Arabian peninsula is home to a sea-turtle population of global importance. Five different species, all of which are endangered, are known to live in its seas. The most common are Green Turtles which nest in their thousands along the beaches of the Arabian Gulf and Oman. It is estimated that between 50,000 and 60,000 Green Turtle egg clutches are laid each year in Oman alone. One of the amazing instincts of sea turtles is their ability to return after several years to exactly the same beach where they hatched. Although they may only nest once every two or three years, they usually return to the same shore. Their nesting site may be just a few hundred yards away from the place where they last made their nest. Scientists are unable to explain how they manage such incredible feats of navigation across the seas with such accuracy. There are few places left in the world where it is safe for turtles to breed, but the beaches of Arabia support large nesting populations. Every effort is being made to ensure that their precious cycle of life is protected, but it is not easy. These creatures cross international boundaries in their life spent at sea, so people from many countries need to work together to ensure their survival.

?

How does a turtle make a safe nest for her eggs?

Turtles mate at sea just off the nesting beach. A female turtle is very nervous about leaving the safety of the sea. As she crawls up above the high tide line to choose a nesting site she pauses frequently, looking out for danger.

After finding a good site she sweeps her front flippers backwards and forwards slowly digging a pit for her body. She digs until it is about thirty centimetres deep, repeatedly stopping to check for danger.

She then concentrates on the egg-chamber. She now uses her back flippers to scoop out the sand to a depth of half a metre, causing her shell to lift from left to right as she digs. Many white, spherical, soft-shelled eggs are dropped into the pit, two or three at a time.

The eggs are covered in thick white mucus which prevents them from drying out. As many as 120 eggs may be laid in the pit. The female will stop laying if the sand is not of the right consistency. The temperature of the sand determines the sex of the baby turtles. Warmer temperatures produce mainly females and cooler temperatures produce males.

The whole nesting process takes about two hours but two-thirds of this time is taken up with covering the eggs to protect them from predators. Drained of energy the female turtle returns to the sea, her interest in her eggs now over. She may nest up to five times in a season at two week intervals.

Approximately 50 days later, the hatchlings emerge from the nest usually at night. The baby turtle breaks free from its egg using an egg tooth on the end of its beak which drops off when the job is completed. Then starts the rush for the sea through the many predators waiting on the shore. Their chances of survival are low but once at the water's edge they swim energetically out to sea where they continue to face many other dangers before becoming adult. Turtles take anywhere between 25 to 50 years to reach maturity and become ready to breed.

Turtles remain at sea for many years, returning to the beach for the nesting season on average only once every five years. It might even be as many as fifteen years before they nest again.

FACTOID

Green Turtles nest in their thousands along the beaches of the Arabian peninsula. It is estimated that between 50,000 and 60,000 Green Turtle egg clutches are laid each year in Oman alone.

Green turtle

What do turtles eat?

Green turtles are herbivores, and feed on algae, seaweeds and sea-grasses. They have bacteria in their stomachs which aids the digestion of cellulose in plant material. They are large turtles with a carapace (upper shell) about a metre long.

The Olive Ridley turtle is a small turtle measuring around 70 cm. This is a rare species but about 100 nest each year on Oman's south-eastern beaches. They feed mainly on crabs, shrimps, jellyfish and sea squirts.

What are the dangers to the eggs and baby turtles?

There are few places left in the world where it is safe for turtles to breed. Many creatures, like those below, prey upon the baby turtles as they make a dash for the ocean. But the beaches of Arabia support large nesting populations, and great efforts are made to protect them.

Hawksbill turtles feed on soft corals, sponges and other coral reef creatures. Their mouths, known as beaks, come to a sharp point and are used to clip their food off the rocks. They are smaller than the Green Turtle, measuring about 80 cm in length. They are considered a highly endangered species.

Man is also responsible for the destruction of turtle habitats. Noise and lights, egg collection, building development and fishing nets all contribute to the disappearance of turtles.

Loggerhead turtles feed on crabs, molluscs and other reef creatures. Measuring about one metre, their carapaces are a light brown colour. Oman is the home of the world's largest nesting population, numbering 30,000. They have been sighted around the Arabian peninsula where they may be foraging for food.

Leatherback turtles are also sighted occasionally in Arabian waters.

SEALIFE — DUGONGS

Mystery surrounds the shy sea-mammal, the dugong, which is one of the most fascinating of marine creatures. Only recently has scientific data been collected about them but in the imagination of sailors they were linked to mythical sirens that looked like mermaids. Stories were told of the singing of the sirens that lured sailors onto the rocks, where they were shipwrecked. In Arabia, they are sometimes known as 'sea-cows' or 'the bride of the sea'. Dugongs are herbivores and totally dependent on a diet of sea-grasses which grow in shallow waters of the Red Sea and the Arabian Gulf. The largest group of dugongs in the world, outside Australia, live in this area. As well as providing food for the dugongs, the sea-grass beds are an important natural resource for the fishing industry as breeding grounds for fish and shrimps. Turtles also feed amongst the grasses. Work is being done to find out more about how sea-grass beds can be protected. Dugongs fill a unique place in the animal kingdom. In many parts of the world they are rapidly disappearing but in this area plans are in place to ensure that care is taken of dugongs and their habitats.

ANTHONY PREEN

ANTHONY PREEN

Some 50 million years ago competition for food on the earth's dry surfaces became too great and some mammals were forced back into the oceans, never to return to land. Dugongs belong to that group. They form the order Sirenia along with their close cousins the manatees. Dugongs live around the edges of the Indian Ocean, in the Gulf, Red Sea and southwest Pacific Ocean, whereas manatees live around the Atlantic Ocean.

ANTHONY PREEN

The paired nostrils on top of the dugong's snout can be seen as it surfaces to breathe air — dolphins and whales have only one breathing hole.

?

Which animals that live on land are relatives of the Dugongs?

Dugongs still have many traits in common with elephants. They are large animals weighing about 400 kilograms and grow to about three metres long. They can be either tan or grey coloured. They have small tusks like miniature versions of the elephant's tusks.

Elephants and dugongs are both herbivores and consume huge quantities of food. They can live for up to seventy years.

Like the ancient elephant, the dugong has kept two incisors.

The skeleton of the Rock hyrax proves its ancestry is similar to the elephant. The Rock hyrax is also a herbivore, like the elephant and dugong.

In many ways a dugong looks like a dolphin except it appears fatter, has a larger tail and a blunt head with a hugely expanded upper lip, or rostral disc. This is covered with sensitive bristles which help the dugong find its preferred food at night and when the water is cloudy.

!

FACTOID

The sea grass on the floor of the ocean has wide empty patches where dugongs have grazed it. It is possible to see from the trails, 15 cm wide and up to several metres long, that dugongs are around.

As they are very shy and difficult to get close to, this is sometimes the only way of knowing that they are living in the area.

Dugongs can use their pectoral fins as props to walk along the seabed.

Their tails, like those of whales and dolphins, move up and down in a horizontal direction to propel them along.

Dugongs rarely reach the fish souqs nowadays. However, the gill nets used by fishermen still catch dugongs accidentally.

Stickers have been given out to fishermen asking them to save dugongs and not kill them.

ANTHONY PREEN

Until recently dugongs played an important part in the life of the coastal people of Arabia. They were hunted for meat, fat and their skins, which made strong leather. Bahrain was the first country of the Arabian peninsula to ban hunting of dugongs.

Posters have been used to request more information about dugongs from anyone who sees them – dead or alive.

ANTHONY PREEN

WANTED

طـلــــوب

معلومـــات عن عرائس البحــر

INFORMATION ON DUGONGS

Dugongs are unusual mammals that live in the shallow waters of the Arabian Gulf and Red Sea. They grow up to 3 metres in length and are brown in colour. They have a large head, and unlike dolphins, they do not have a fin on their back. They are docile and feed on the leaves and roots of sea grasses.

Dugongs are very slow breeders and are vulnerable to pollution and drowning in nets. As a result they are now very rare and are in danger of becoming extinct.

Yon can assist research to help the dugong...

If you see any Dugong - Alive, dead or even decomposed:

Please Contact : Mr. ANTHONY PREEN
M.E.P.A.
P. O. Box 117
Dhahran Airport
Tel. 8910737
8981980 ext. 219 (After 2:30 PM)

M E P A

Presidency of Meteorology & Environmental Protection Administration
EASTERN PROVINCE

SEALIFE — CETACEANS: BALEEN WHALES

Living in the watery world beneath the sea are the group of animals called cetaceans. All whales and dolphins belong to this group. Each species has its own individual appearance and behaviour but they all need to breathe air at the surface of the ocean. There are eighty known species belonging to this group world-wide, and many of them occur off the shores of the Arabian peninsula. Only in recent years has data been collected about whales and dolphins in this part of the world. There are plenty of questions about their way of life that are still unanswered. Like many other creatures, cetaceans have a struggle to survive at sea, where man's activities pose a threat to their environment. It is of great importance that we work to understand their needs and protect these amazing creatures.

The first sign that there is a whale in the area is its blow.

s the whale urfaces a ixture of otale air and water vapour is blown into the air.

How many different kinds of whales and dophins live in Arabian waters?

All these species are known to have swum in Arabian waters but some of them are very rare. The only way we know they are there is by their bones, which are sometimes washed up on the beaches. However, some of the species can often be seen swimming in Arabian waters in large numbers.

Baleen Whales	Toothed Whales, Dolphins and Porpoises	
Blue whale	Sperm whale	Cuvier's beaked whale
Fin whale	Dwarf sperm whale	Bottlenose dolphin
Bryde's whale	Killer whale	Striped dolphin
Humpback whale	Finless porpoise	Indo Pacific Humpback dolphin
Minke whale	Melon headed whale	Risso's dolphin
	Pygmy killer whale	Rough Toothed dolphin
	False killer whale	Common dolphin
		Spotted dolphin
		Spinner dolphin

Blue whales are by far the largest animals to have ever lived on earth, dwarfing even the extinct dinosaurs. A large one measures 25 metres and can gulp 60 tonnes of water and food in a single mouthful.

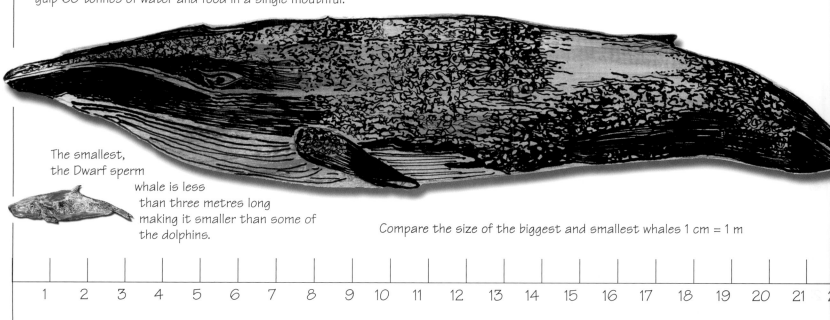

The smallest, the Dwarf sperm whale is less than three metres long making it smaller than some of the dolphins.

Compare the size of the biggest and smallest whales 1 cm = 1 m

1 2 3 4 5 6 7 8 9 10 11 12 13 14 15 16 17 18 19 20 21

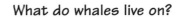

What do whales live on?

A whale has a daily problem of finding enough food to feed its huge body. Differences in the way that whales feed separates the species into two main groups.

Some whales have teeth and are called toothed whales. This group includes all the dolphins and porpoises. They feed on fish and squid. Their razor-sharp teeth enable them to hold onto their slippery prey.

Other whales do not have teeth but feed using sieve-like bristles that hang from the upper jaw called **baleen**. These whales can only eat very small fish, such as sardines. Nothing bigger than an orange can pass down their throats. They also eat the **zooplankton**, which are minute creatures present in huge numbers in the sea. The Blue whale consumes four million of these tiny creatures in one day.

Baleen whales have huge pleated throats. The pleats act like a concertina and expand to hold vast quantities of food-laden water. When the whale is not eating, the throat looks flat and its pleats cannot be seen.

Another name for these baleen whales is rorquals. This word means 'furrowed'. Furrows are deep lines that are ploughed into fields and this name is given to the whales because of their pleated throats.

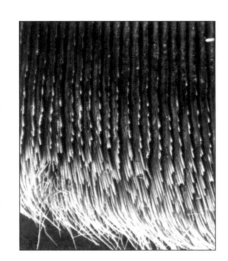

The longest baleen plates may be one metre long and 50 cm wide.

When water is taken into the whale's mouth it snaps shut and the water is forced out through bristles, leaving the small creatures behind. The tongue sweeps the food that has been collected on the bristles into its throat.

By this method the largest creature in the world is able to feed on some of the smallest creatures.

A group of whales is called a pod.

This Hump-backed whale (*right*) is leaping into the air after being rescued from fishing nets off the coast of Oman. When it breaches a whale leaps into the air, usually two or three times but this animal leapt 150 times to celebrate its freedom. The record number of leaps is thought to be about 200.

SEALIFE — CETACEANS: TOOTHED WHALES AND DOLPHINS

Toothed whales and dolphins swim superbly through the water, driven by up and down sweeps of their horizontal tails. There are sixteen known species of toothed cetaceans living in the coastal waters of Arabia. Although the species look very different, they belong in the same group because they all have teeth. They swim at great speeds to catch their prey which may be fish, squid or even other cetaceans. The killer whale is the fastest, reaching speeds of over 55 kilometres an hour. Dolphins swim so rapidly they can be seen taking off and leaping into the air. They follow boats in an inquisitive manner, and their intelligent smiling faces make them very attractive to us. We are fascinated by the mystery surrounding these creatures of the deep and the marvellous ways they are adapted to live there.

Dorsal fin

Streamlined body

Blow hole

The main features of all toothed cetaceans are shown on this dolphin.

Blow hole through which it breathes. It holds its breath all the time it is underwater. A Sperm whale may stay down for well over an hour.

Flippers

Huge muscles make up one third of its back, and propel it along.

Beak

Ultrasound is used as part of their sonar system which they use to find their way around and locate fish. They send out clicking noises and listen for returning echoes.

!

FACTOID
Sperm whales are the largest of toothed whales. The thick teeth of the huge Sperm whale can grow to 20 cm in length and weigh a kilogram each.

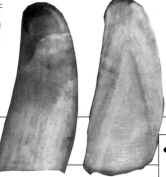

Ambergris (a sticky black substance) comes from the gut of the Sperm whale. An irritation to the gut, caused by the whale's diet of cuttlefish, produces ambergris. Oil of ambergris is used in the making of *bakhoor*, sweet smelling incense cakes. Synthetic ambergris is sometimes used also.

?

Do you beleive it is possible to kill your dinner by sound only?

It is thought that the Sperm whale may be able to do just that. By firing extremely loud sounds at squid, they are stunned or killed. Using sonar signals as it dives, the Sperm whale can locate and kill a giant squid up to ten metres across.

On this skeleton of a cetacean the flippers clearly show how similar these bones are to hands of humans.

Whales and dolphins are social animals. They like to work as members of a group.

Dolphins use lots of different methods for hunting but will always hunt together. They make a circle around the fish so they cannot swim away. One or two of the group swim into the circle and grab the frightened fish while the rest stay round the outside waiting for their turn to eat.

A dolphin can starve if it becomes isolated from its group and has no other dolphins to fish with.

Horizontal tail

The tail goes up and down as the dolphin swims. The ends of the tail are called flukes.

Unlike cetaceans, fish have a vertical tail (*above*) that goes from side to side as it swims.

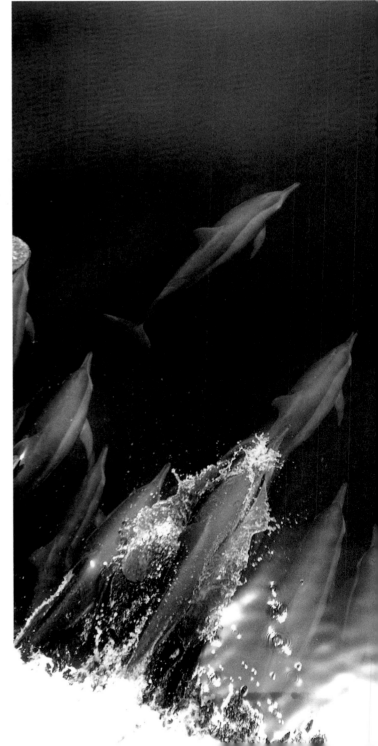

All whales and dolphins give birth to fully formed babies. The baby is born tail first. If it was born head first it would drown. The mother, helped by other members of the group, nudges the baby to the surface for its first gasp of air.

The mother feeds her baby with milk and teaches it everything it needs to know. It may stay with her for several years.

SEALIFE — CORAL REEFS

The coral reefs of the Red Sea are among the most famous in the world. Coral reefs are also found on many coastlines of the Arabian peninsula. A coral reef is made up of hundreds of thousands of coral animals called polyps, which work together to defend themselves, share food and spawn their eggs. The polyp is the living part of the coral reef growing inside a rock like skeleton. The polyp, like any other animal, eventually dies and stony skeletons of the dead corals gradually build up into a thick layer which forms the main body of the reef. New polyps settle and grow on the outside layer. Coral grows in many different shapes, sizes and colours. Tropical corals, such as those seen in Arabia, need warm and clean seas in which to grow. Sunlight passes through the water to reach the tiny animals at the centre of the coral. Young coral larvae can travel through the sea for hundreds of kilometres, but once settled on a hard surface are not able to move from this time onwards. As many other sea creatures are attracted to the reef to feed and breed the whole reef becomes a rich and beautiful habitat for sea life.

Different types of coral have their own names. Some reefs are entirely made up of one type of coral. The reef attracts many colourful fish that graze on the outside layers of the corals.

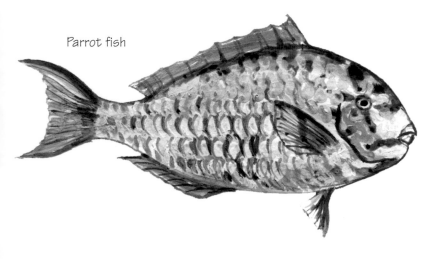

Parrot fish

Batfish

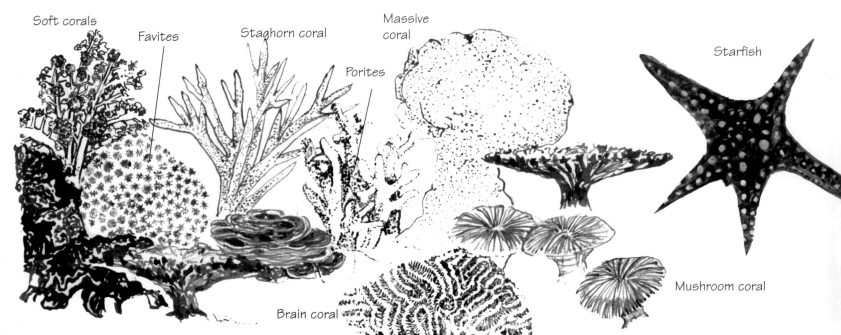

Soft corals

Favites

Staghorn coral

Porites

Massive coral

Starfish

Brain coral

Mushroom coral

Forming artificial reefs

Some corals like beaches with crashing waves. Some like a rocky shore with clear, still water but they all prefer a solid base to grow on. Long stretches of the coastline of Arabia are sandy. One way a coral reef can be formed in these areas is by artificial means, such as sinking old ships. Artificial reefs have also been created by sinking concrete blocks. In three months fifty per cent of the reef is covered in simple, green plant life called algae. The algae attracts barnacles, sponges, coral heads and oysters. Reef fish are also drawn to the reef. By the end of the first year the artificial reefs are totally covered with animal life.

After three months   After one year

?

How do corals eat?

Hard corals feed in two ways. First the polyp uses stinging cells in its tentacles to catch plankton in the water and feed them into its mouth. It looks like a small tree with its branches swaying in the wind as its tentacles reach out for food. The polyps only extend their tentacles to feed at night.

Secondly, algae that live inside the polyp use sunlight, carbon dioxide and water to make food by the process called photosynthesis. This food is used by the polyp. Waste from the polyp is used by the algae. This relationship between algae and polyps, means that corals can survive where water contains few nutrients.

All that is seen in the day time is the rock-like skeleton. The skeleton is formed of limestone around the base of the coral polyp. They grow upon this skeleton.

Soft corals are made up of a soft fleshy body on which the polyps live. They can feed at any time. They defend themselves from animals trying to eat them by producing toxic chemicals. They have many wonderful shapes and colours.

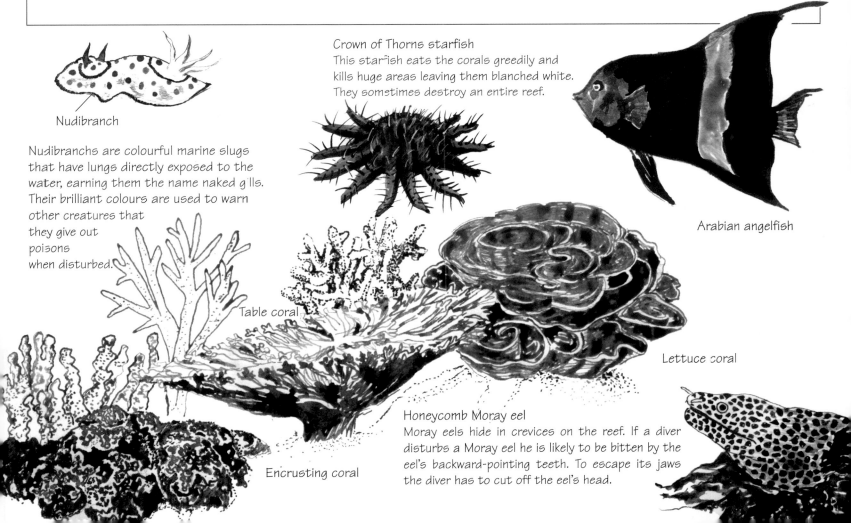

Nudibranch

Nudibranchs are colourful marine slugs that have lungs directly exposed to the water, earning them the name naked gills. Their brilliant colours are used to warn other creatures that they give out poisons when disturbed.

Crown of Thorns starfish
This starfish eats the corals greedily and kills huge areas leaving them blanched white. They sometimes destroy an entire reef.

Arabian angelfish

Table coral

Lettuce coral

Honeycomb Moray eel
Moray eels hide in crevices on the reef. If a diver disturbs a Moray eel he is likely to be bitten by the eel's backward-pointing teeth. To escape its jaws the diver has to cut off the eel's head.

Encrusting coral

SEALIFE – DANGERS IN THE SEA

Biting, stinging and venomous spines are all methods used by sea creatures to protect themselves. They are not normally aggressive if left alone but some marine animals have very dangerous weapons they can use if threatened. Man does not form part of the food chain for marine creatures in the seas around the Arabian peninsula but injuries can happen if marine life is trapped or trodden on. The camouflage of some creatures prevents them being noticed until it is too late to avoid them. Even brushing against jellyfish or creatures that live among coral reefs can result in painful stings or wounds. The mention of the word 'shark' is enough to bring fear to many people but the shark's bad reputation is not deserved. It is a curious creature that is attracted by vibrations in the sea but only if the smell of blood accompanies the movements in the water is it thought to be aggressive.

!

FACTOID

Toxic red-coloured water, known as red tide, caused by a concentration of algae, is deadly to some marine creatures. It is thought that dolphins, dugongs, turtles and fish may be killed by ingesting it. People vomit if they swallow it.

?

Are there many poisonous creatures in the seas of Arabia?

Some species living among coral reefs are the most venomous creatures in Arabian waters. Scorpionfish, Lionfish and Stonefish belong to the same family and an encounter with any one of them is potentially very dangerous. Even corals themselves are much more treacherous than their beautiful appearance would have us think.

A Stonefish is a bottom dweller which lives its entire life in one area seldom moving more than a few centimetres at a time. It has a big, upturned mouth into which it sucks its prey. It is perfectly camouflaged on the sea floor. Its venom causes intense pain and it can be fatal.

A Lionfish has beautiful fins but also possesses venomous spines along its back which are harmful to man. Although it usually defends itself with its spine, it has been known to twist its body to jab a victim as it attacks. Its venom results in pain, weakness, sickness and difficulty in breathing.

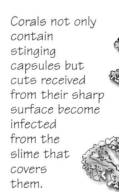

Corals not only contain stinging capsules but cuts received from their sharp surface become infected from the slime that covers them.

Jellyfish float where the currents take them, eating whatever comes their way. They belong to the same family as sea anemones and corals. Tentacles hang down from the main part of their body and are coated with stinging capsules called nematocysts. They deposit poison on the skin of anyone touching them.

A harmless monster

Whale shark

The Whale shark is not only the largest shark, measuring up to 12 metres in length, but the biggest fish in the sea. It is quite harmless, feeding on zoo plankton and other small creatures. It moves very gracefully.

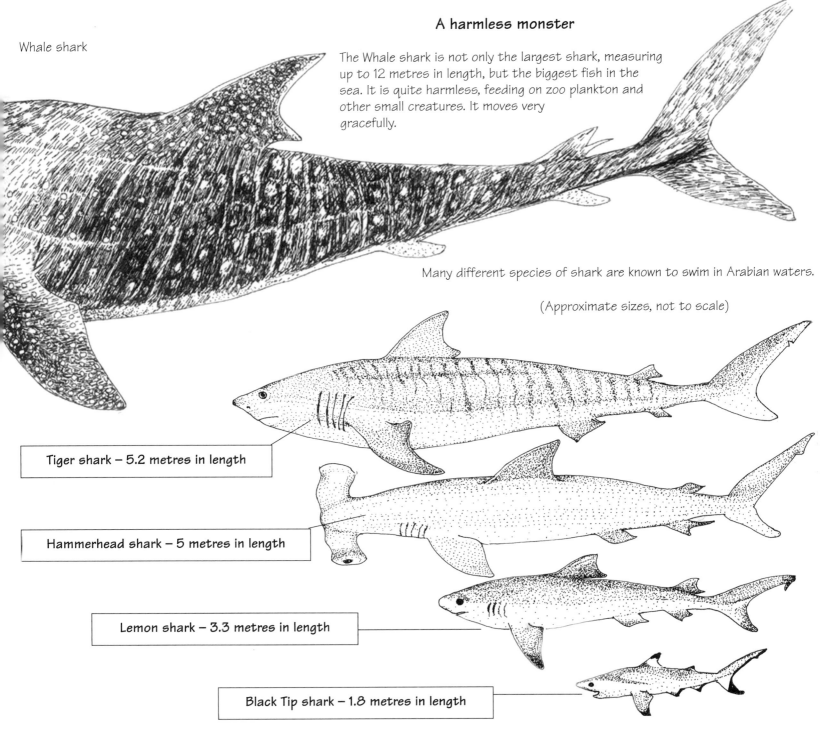

Many different species of shark are known to swim in Arabian waters.

(Approximate sizes, not to scale)

Tiger shark – 5.2 metres in length

Hammerhead shark – 5 metres in length

Lemon shark – 3.3 metres in length

Black Tip shark – 1.8 metres in length

The teeth of most sharks are in many rows. At rest, only the first row of teeth stick upwards and the others are turned inwards. However, when the shark bites, it erects all the rows. The teeth in the reserve rows move forward to replace the teeth in the front row every 10 days or so. Unlike other fish, most species of shark give birth to a completely formed baby. Others lay eggs in a horny case called a mermaid's purse.

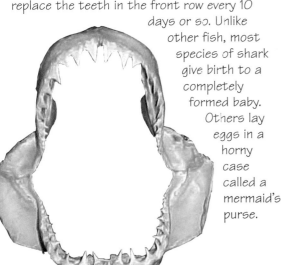

These fishermen have caught a shark in their nets.

Kite-shaped stingrays belong to the same family as sharks. Their tails have one or more spines which contain poisonous venom. They lie motionless on the sand, often in shallow water, and if trodden on they slash defensively with their tail. Fishermen fear them. When they catch rays, they leave them on the beach to die.

Stingray

INSECT LIFE

The insect world contains more members than any other single group of animals. Insects are remarkably adaptable and live everywhere on the Arabian peninsula, even in the most scorching parts of the desert. They belong to a group called arthropods. They have a hard, protective skeleton that is on the outside of their body. They do not have a backbone so they are invertebrates. They have six jointed legs, and most species have wings. In beetles the front pair of wings are like a hard case that lies over the top of the hind wings, which are used for flying. Insects are sometimes thought of as pests, bringing dirt and disease to man, but they are vital for our survival.

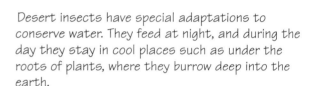

Praying mantis

Desert insects have special adaptations to conserve water. They feed at night, and during the day they stay in cool places such as under the roots of plants, where they burrow deep into the earth.

Very little moisture is lost from their bodies. A tough external skeleton is covered with wax to help insects retain water.

Useful jobs insects do

Break down decomposing material and return it to the soil as valuable nutrients.

They are an important food source for other creatures.

They keep the insect population under control by feeding on other insects.

They help to pollinate flowers of food crops.

Black Beetles

Mouth Parts

Some insects have biting and chewing mouth parts. They are predators, which means that they attack and feed on other living creatures.

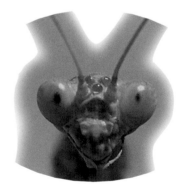

The front legs of the Praying mantis are well developed to catch and hold their prey. They usually eat other insects but can even take small lizards. The male must be very wary when he is mating. The female is quite likely to eat him! She needs the protein to nourish her eggs.

Everywhere you go in the desert you seem to notice these beetles. There are more than 300 diferent kinds of them and they are called Darkling beetles. Their size varies from minute to 4 cm. Their hind wings are fused together so they can no longer fly and are covered with wax to prevent water loss.

They use their speed to run away from enemies. Although they are mostly harmless some of them can send out nasty liquids, which smell and taste bad, to make sure they aren't a nice dinner.

Domino beetle   Oil beetle

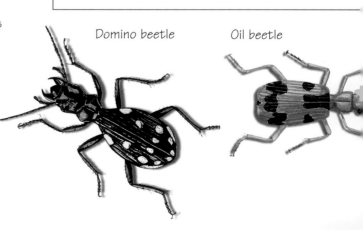

How are insects born?

Advanced forms of insects, like the fly, and butterfly go through the unusual life cycle known as metamorphosis.

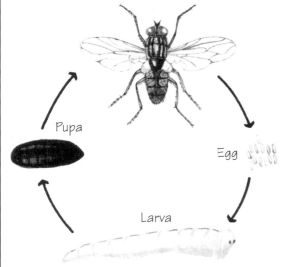

Pupa

Egg

Larva

When the larva enters the pupa stage the whole body changes completely before an adult emerges.

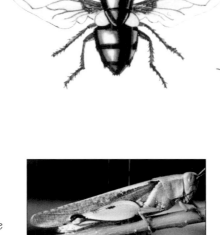

Locusts and grasshoppers, like many other insects go through incomplete metamorphosis.

Adult

Egg

Nymph (instar)

Nymph (instar)

Little locusts and grasshoppers look like their parents, only smaller. As they grow they shed their skin, getting a little larger each time. It takes five to eight skin changes before reaching adult size.

Other insects have specially adapted mouths to suck up their food in a liquid form. They can either be blood sucking or plant sucking.

Palm trees are attacked by a weevil that bores up into the trunk. Water cannot pass up the tree so it dies. This weevil was introduced to Arabia probably amongst some date palms, and has become a pest! It has spread through many areas.

Ladybird

Beetles are not always black. Metallic greens and reds are common. Colour is often a warning to predators that they are toxic and distasteful to eat.

FACTOID!

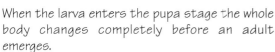

The Scarab, or Dung beetle (*left*) follows herds of camels and other livestock. It shapes and rolls a ball of dung across the desert, searching for a place to excavate a tunnel in which to bury the dung. Having buried the dung, the beetle lays a single egg and seals the entrance to the tunnel. Larvae hatch out in a safe place, with all the food they need nearby.

At night, in the camel camps, the ground comes alive with the beetles carrying off the dung balls.

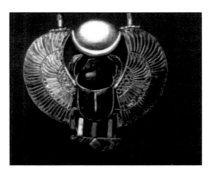

The Scarab beetle was sacred to the ancient Egyptians, and was often used as a motif in jewellery and ornamentation. The picture (*left*) shows Tutarkamun's 'Necklace of the Sun on the Eastern Horizon'; gold, lapis azuli and carnelian.

FACTOID!

The larva of the Antlion fly is only 2mm long, but it is a very clever hunter. It digs a cone shaped pit in loose sand and sits at the bottom. It is warned of tiny insects approaching by loose grains of sand rolling into the pit. The antlion larva then springs into action. It throws sand at its prey until the creature loses its balance and tumbles into the pit where it gets eaten.

LIVING WITH INSECTS

Sadly, the insects we dislike most are the ones that seem to enjoy sharing our homes. Although most insects have a useful role to play on our planet, a few of them are pests. They can carry diseases, destroy our crops and gardens, and eat into the wooden parts of our buildings. We declare war on the insects, spraying them and their breeding grounds with chemicals to kill them. Not only does this cost a lot of money, but the chemical sprays pollute our atmosphere and our water.

'Foggers' (insecticide sprays) are used in the fight against mosquitoes.

? Why is there a war against mosquitoes in Arabia?

In some parts of Arabia where there is regular rainfall and plenty of vegetation, malaria-carrying mosquitoes manage to breed. Mosquito larvae (right) live in fresh water. Sometimes the small amount caught in the leaves of a banana plant is sufficient for them to survive.

It is the female mosquito that carries malaria. She needs human blood for her eggs to mature. Malaria causes repeated bouts of fever in humans, and can even result in death. The male mosquito is harmless and feeds on nectar.

The mouth parts of a mosquito are extremely sharp so we are not aware when it pierces our skin and sucks our blood. As it sucks our blood, it injects us with saliva which contains anti-coagulents. These stop the blood from clotting, so that it flows freely into the mosquito's gut. The mixture causes an allergic reaction, making the bite itch.

? Which creatures are helpful in getting rid of mosquitoes?

A type of fish called a Tilapia (left) has been introduced into pools and wadis to try to control the mosquito larvae. They are helpful in that they destroy the larvae, but unfortunately they are larger than the native fish and may eventually destroy them also. They are capable of surviving when the water in the wadi dries up by burying their eggs in the damp mud. When another rainfall fills up the wadi with water again, the eggs hatch out.

Like other lizards, geckos (right) help in the fight against mosquitoes. They are nocturnal, and dart out from their hiding places with great speed to catch their prey. The pads on their feet allow them to run across vertical walls and the ceilings of our houses.

The leaves of a banana tree can collect enough water for the mosquito to lay its eggs. Banana trees are also sprayed with insecticides to kill the mosquito larvae.

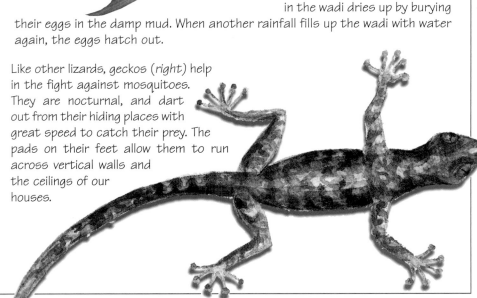

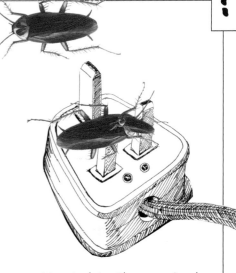

What do cockroaches like to eat?

Some insects like to share our food. They thrive on dirt and spread germs and bacteria.

The cockroach is a fast-moving creature of the night. Fossil remains show that they existed 300 million years ago. They are so flat that even the smallest crack or crevice seems wide enough for them to slide through. Although they prefer to run when startled, they can fly when they need to move to new sites.

Cockroaches are attracted to the organic glue used to stick circuitry in modern electrical appliances. They like the mild heat provided by the current flowing through appliances, such as telephones and televisions.

A cockroach will eat any organic matter. Dirt and grease found in drains are its favourite foods.

A cockroach is omnivorous, which means it will eat all kinds of food. This is one reason why cockroaches have flourished for millions of years.

Flies

Flies can only ingest liquids. To feed on solid food, flies have to vomit on it first so that the enzymes in their digestive juices break down the food to a digestible state. Their sponge-like mouth parts then soak up the liquified food. They leave germs and bacteria on our food, giving us diarrhoea and stomach aches.

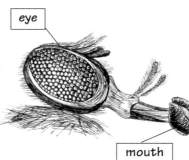

eye

mouth

The magnified mouth of a fly.

Locusts

The sight of a swarm of locusts brings fear to farmers. In a few minutes, they can destroy the vegetation of a whole area. In the past, when people lived in palm frond houses, locusts could ruin their homes. Locusts only swarm when they become overcrowded and large numbers need to migrate to another place to search for food. They even change their appearance, becoming darker in colour. Their wings become longer and stronger as they get ready to fly off.

Why do termites cause problems to humans?

In Arabia, many homes are attacked by termites. They live on dead or decaying wood. They have protozoa in their stomachs which break down cellulose in the wood. They do a useful job eating into dead trees in the wild so they are returned to the soil as nutrients. However, they can completely destroy a house by eating away at its wooden parts. Termites live in colonies with several different castes that have different jobs to do.

The king and queen are the primary reproducers of the colony. They have been known to live together for as long as fifty years. The queen can grow to as much as ten centimetres long as her abdomen swells up with eggs.

The worker caste looks after the royal couple, tends to the eggs and young, forages for food, feeds the soldiers and builds and maintains the nest.

The soldiers defend the nest. There are two types, Major soldiers and Minor soldiers.

Winged adult

Minor soldier

Major soldier

INSECTS — BUTTERFLIES AND MOTHS

Butterflies and moths are all insects that belong to a family called Lepidoptera, which comes from the Greek words for 'scales' and 'wings'. There are thought to be about 20,000 species of butterflies in the world, but only a small group of them live in Arabia. This is because most butterflies live on plants, and the arid climate does not always provide them with the food they need. The size of an adult butterfly can alter depending on how much food its larva has been able to eat. It is much larger if conditions are good. Many butterflies and moths migrate to find the best conditions for laying their eggs. Each species needs to spread out over as wide an area as possible so that bad weather does not affect them all. Although butterflies and moths appear very fragile insects, they are capable of migrating for hundreds of miles. The life-cycle of the butterfly involves complete metamorphosis (see insect life page, 141).

Frequently seen butterflies in Arabia are the Plain Tiger, the Lime butterfly and the Swallowtail.

Lime butterfly

Citrus fruit, including lime, are the food that Lime butterfly caterpillars prefer. The female butterfly searches the trees carefully for fresh shoots on which she lays one egg on each leaf to make sure the caterpillar has plenty to eat.

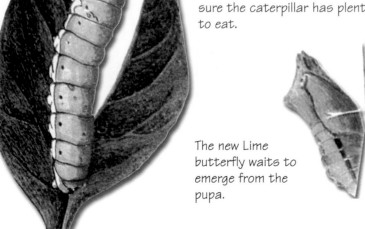

The new Lime butterfly waits to emerge from the pupa.

FACTOID

!

Plants known as milkweeds are the preferred food of Plain Tiger caterpillars. Sodom's Apple is a milkweed, and a favourite place for the Plain Tiger butterfly to lay her eggs.

The pupa hangs underneath the leaf. Sometimes they are a bright green, sometimes brown, depending which colour will camouflage them the best. A new Plain Tiger butterfly emerges from the pupa to start the life cycle all over again.

The milkweed plant contains poisons which get stored in the body of the Plain Tiger. Birds soon get to know that they are toxic and not good to eat.

The **Diadem butterfly** mimics the colours of the Plain Tiger. It does not eat the milkweeds, so it is not poisonous, but predators are deceived into thinking that it is. They do not attack it.

Why is the diet of the Leopard Butterfly unusual?

Not all caterpillars eat plants. The group called Lycaenidae, Blue butterflies, of which the Leopard butterfly is a member, have a very unusual diet.

Plain Tiger butterfly

A Rhinoceros beetle makes cavities in the stumps of old leaf fronds from the palm tree. Ants visit the trees to get nectar.

The Leopard butterfly lays her eggs in the cavities that the beetle has made. She chooses ones that are near to the ant nests.

When the eggs become larvae the ants are attracted to them and carry them into their nest. They like the sugary secretions that come from the legs of the larvae.

The ants rear the butterfly larvae as if they were ant larvae. The butterfly larvae appear to feed on the ant larvae in the nest.

Is it a butterfly or a moth?

The caterpillars are not any help in telling the difference between butterflies and moths. They come in a great variety of shapes, sizes and colours but there is no single way to know whether they are butterfly or moth larvae.

The body structure of adult insects are the best way to tell the difference between a butterfly and a moth.

The antennae of the butterfly end in a club shape.

The body of the butterfly is much smaller than the fatter, furry body of the moth. The wings are often more colourful than a moth's wings.

A butterfly flies by day and settles with its wings upright, folded over its back.

The moth's wings are stretched out flat when it settles.

The antennae of the moth are feathered or straight.

These two caterpillars look very different. They are both the larvae of moths.

Great superstition surrounds the Death's-Head Hawkmoth because of the markings on its back which look like a skull. Both the larvae and the moth can make a squeaking noise.

INSECTS – BEES, WASPS AND ANTS

Bees, wasps and ants all belong to the same family called Hymenoptera, which is part of the insect group. Although they are members of the same family, they have very different habits. They are sometimes solitary, living by themselves, but usually they live in well-organised colonies, where each member of the colony has a job to do. The adult members look after the legless larvae, who do not move out of the nest until they are adult.

Hornet digger

Why are wasps so dangerous to other insects?

Wasps prey on small creatures, such as spiders, for their living food store. They paralyse the bodies with their sting, and suck the juices from their victims at a later time.

The Potter wasp builds a nest from sand or mud, mixed with saliva. This bakes hard in the sun, and looks like a small pot, hanging singly from walls or rocks. It lays one egg inside and fills the nest with paralysed prey, such as caterpillars, for the larvae to feed on.

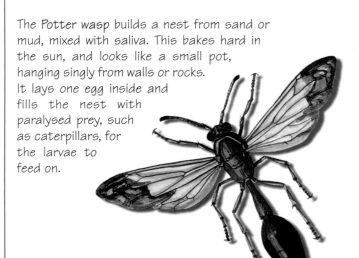

The Paper wasp with its long dangly yellow legs can be very aggressive. They build the nests from wood, which they chew into pulp.

Some wasps that live on the stony plains hunt spiders. The wasp paralyses a spider by stinging it. They dig a burrow and put the spider inside. The wasp then lays one egg next to the spider which acts as a living food store for its developing larva to eat. It then seals up the entrance.

Why are ants important to the cycle of life?

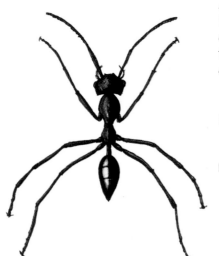

Ants are the scavengers of the desert. They perform an important job by eating the dead bodies of other creatures. Many desert creatures also eat the ants, so they are a valuable food source. There are around 300 different species of ants on the Arabian peninsula.

brought to Arabia from sting. Some people are it can even be fatal. They clements.

The largest ant is the black Desert Giant ant which measures 2 cm. It is harmless.

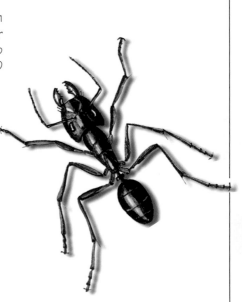

Why are bees such useful insects?

Honey produced by Honey bees is important to people living in Arabia as a source of food. Bees also help pollinate crops as they go from flower to flower, collecting nectar and pollen.

The wild desert, or mountain bee, builds its honeycomb in places difficult to reach such as high trees, or caves. This makes the collection of the honey a very dangerous task.

FACTOID

Eighty per cent of fruits and vegetables are pollinated by honey bees. 20 per cent by other insects, and the wind.

The honeycomb

Although many plants are visited by the bees, acacia and sidr trees are the most frequently visited for nectar and pollen collection.

Sidr

Acacia

What is the traditional way of making a beehive in Arabia?

There are two types of hive. A traditional hive is used in Oman and southern Arabia. It is made from the hollowed out logs of palm trees, or clay tubes. Pieces of trunk or tubes are laid horizontally, one on top of the other. Sometimes as many as 200 hives are kept in the same place.

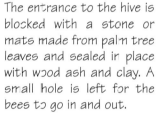

The entrance to the hive is blocked with a stone or mats made from palm tree leaves and sealed in place with wood ash and clay. A small hole is left for the bees to go in and out.

Each day the bees make many trips outside the hive. Between 7-15 trips are made to collect nectar and slightly fewer to collect pollen but as many as 100 trips are made to collect water. The water is evaporated to control the temperature inside the hive. It must not go higher than 34.5°C.

To make a new hive an incubator comb containing a queen is fixed inside the palm log with two wooden sticks placed each side of the comb to hold it in position.

A modern hive is made from a wooden box, with the advantage that honeycombs can be easily removed and inspected. There are usually ten frames inside the box. Both types of hive must be placed near to the food plants of the bee. The honey of the acacia is harvested in May. The honey of the sidr is harvested in November and December.

Which insects prey on the bees in their hives?

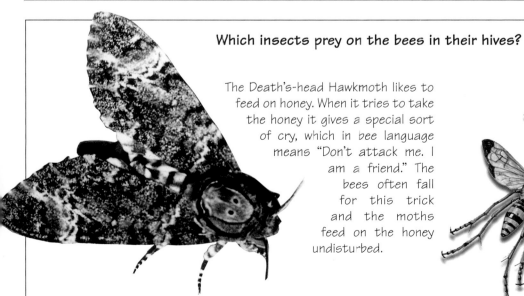

The Death's-head Hawkmoth likes to feed on honey. When it tries to take the honey it gives a special sort of cry, which in bee language means "Don't attack me. I am a friend." The bees often fall for this trick and the moths feed on the honey undisturbed.

The Oriental wasp preys on the Honey bee and is known to have completely taken over some hives. Samsun Ants also prey on Honey Bees.

SPIDERS AND SCORPIONS

Spiders and scorpions form a group called arachnids. They are not insects, although they also belong to the arthropod family with hard external skeletons and jointed legs. Their bodies are in two parts, with the head and thorax fused together and an abdomen. In scorpions the abdomen includes the tail with a stinger that contains venom. They have eight legs, but no wings or antennae. Scorpions are among the earliest land animals and have existed on earth for 400 million years. They are all nocturnal and have their own territory.

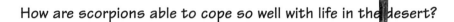

How are scorpions able to cope so well with life in the desert?

Scorpions are long lived. Their surface is waterproof, so they do not lose moisture from their bodies. They can survive for longer than a year without food. Their only source of water comes from the prey they eat.

They live in burrows in the sand and soil or hide under rocks, only emerging at night. This helps them cope with the most intense heat.

Some common scorpions are large and black. Other species that live in the desert are brown or sandy in colour with a small and slender body.

A sting in the tail!
The venom in the stinger is used to subdue the scorpion's prey. It is often held above the body in defence. A sting is very painful to humans but not usually fatal.

The pedipalps, or pincers, are used to hold their prey while it is sucked dry.

At night the scorpion glows with a fluorescent light. Its exoskeleton reacts to ultra violet light.

The scorpion is a very good mother. Her babies are born live and soon after birth they clamber onto her back. They can rely on her to protect them.

Scorpions can sense if their prey is nearby by smell and vibrations on the ground. Underneath their bodies they have a pair of pectines, which are like combs. These can sense the slightest movement.

FACTOID!

There are almost 40 different species or sub-species of scorpions in Arabia. More is being found out about them every year as further studies are carried out.

What are the different ways spiders use to catch their prey?

Spiders are adapted to many different environments and lifestyles on land, in the air or on water. All spiders catch live prey to eat. Some of them build webs to catch their prey. Other spiders roam freely, attacking unsuspecting insects, or hide and wait until their prey comes too close. A hole in the ground, a crack in the rocks or even the centre of a colourful flower can hide a spider.

Champion jumpers – Jumping spider
One species of spider that does not need a web to catch its prey is the Jumping spider (*right*). These spiders can even catch insects in flight. They have very good eyesight and an intense stare.

Wolf spiders are also free roaming and lie in wait to run down their prey. They are active by both day and night.

A Crab spider takes on the same colour as the flower in which it is hiding.

This Argrobe or Orb Web spider makes a web which can be as much as 1 metre across. The centre of the web may be decorated with white zig-zag patterns of silk.

This spider would make a tasty meal for a bird or a mammal. When the spider senses danger it can vibrate the web rapidly, which makes it very difficult for other creatures to take aim and catch it.

A dangerous spider – the Redback of Arabia spider is closely related to the Black Widow and Australian Redback. The female carries her egg sacs with her. Each egg sac can contain fifty or more babies.

Look out for Redbacks in your garden or garage. They have potent venom if they bite you.

This fearsome looking creature is a Camel spider. It can be either sandy coloured or black. It is not a true spider as it has neither spinnerets to make silk nor poison to paralyse its prey. The thick and hairy touch organs on either side of its head are its pedipalps. They are used for grasping its prey. Its food is digested inside its body.

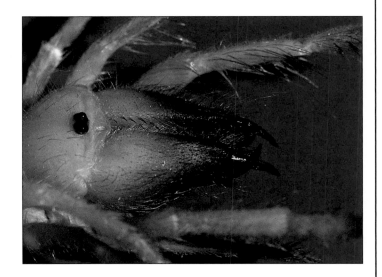

A close-up of the Camel spider's jaws shows how a nasty wound could result from its bite.

WADI CREATURES

A wadi is a river bed. Some are almost always dry, while others are flowing with water all year round. The water in the wadi is alive with creatures specially adapted to spend their lives in or near fresh water. Some insects spend their entire life in the water. Other insects, such as dragonflies and mosquitoes, need a supply of fresh water to complete their life-cycle. Some insects are carnivorous, hunting down other water creatures for food. Other water insects are vegetarian, living entirely on plants and algae. Toads live near the water laying their eggs, known as spawn, in it. Fish are plentiful and many of them are able to survive the hot summer months in small, isolated pools of water that lie between the rocks.

Toads have excellent camouflage that helps them hide among the stones of the wadi. They are amphibians. Their eggs are laid into the water and the larvae, known as tadpoles, breathe through gills. As they develop into adults, they grow legs and lungs. They leave the water and live mostly on land.

The toad's diet consists mainly of insects and its large mouth acts as an excellent trap for them. Some of the insects dive underwater to escape being caught, and the toad can pursue them below the surface. The toad has been known to eat other toads. It can open its mouth so wide it can easily take the whole head of another toad into it.

Saqvigny's Tree frog lives in moist parts of western Arabia.

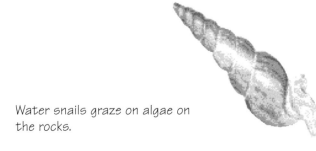

Bahrain's Marsh frog.

Wadi fish are generally small, but some can grow to about 12 cm long. Wadi pools are crowded with different species of fish camouflaged to protect them from birds and snakes.

Water snails graze on algae on the rocks.

What insects can be found in the wadi water?

Dragonflies are powerful flyers, catching insects to eat in midair. However, the greatest part of their lives is spent below the surface of the water. Their eggs are laid into the water and their young, known as nymphs, develop on the wadi bed.

The nymphs of both species are very aggressive predators. They have a huge lower lip, known as a mask. When the nymph spots its prey, it uses a hinge mechanism to extend its lip to a much greater length than in its usual resting position. As well as their diet of other water insects, they sometimes attack small fish and tadpoles.

The mask when resting

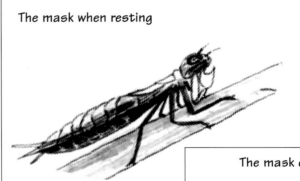

The bright colours of dragonflies and damselflies catch our eye as they skim and dart over the water.

The nymphs crawl up rocks or reeds out of the water to moult. Their skin splits down the centre and they emerge as adults, ready to fly off immediately.

Adult dragonflies do not need to stay near water which is why they are seen in hot, dry places. They are known to migrate over hundreds of miles.

The mask extended

Fish have gills to breathe under the water, but insects who make the water their home adopt different methods of taking oxygen with them as they swim underneath the surface of the water.

The Water scorpion is not really a scorpion, although it looks like one. It has a long tail divided into two hollow tubes through which it breathes. The air it collects is stored under its wings until it is needed.

Water boatmen swim in great numbers on the surface of the water.

The water beetle and mosquito larvae collect air through a snorkel-like tubes before sinking to the wadi bed.

Dragonfly nymphs have internal gills so do not need to come to the surface to breathe. They may live in the wadi water for several years before becoming adults. Damselfly nymphs breathe through tail-like gills.

The Diving beetle survives by collecting air on the surface and storing it under its wing covers. The supply of air lasts the beetle about ten minutes before it needs to return to the srface for more air.

FACTOID

Leeches live on a diet of blood. They suck it from a host fish. In the past doctors used leeches to cure certain ailments. A yellow leech lives on the wadi bed.

MODERN

ARABIA

MODERN
ARABIA

DISCOVERY OF OIL — EARLY EXPLORATION

In ancient times, people collected seepages of oil that came through the sand and seabed to make their wooden boats waterproof. These were early signs that oil was present in Arabia. However, it was not until the middle of the twentieth century that anyone realised the enormous reserves of oil that lay beneath the deserts and seas. The way of life for the people of Arabia changed so dramatically after its discovery that the pre-oil and post-oil times seem like two different worlds. Oil was called the new 'black gold'. Twentieth century inventions such as cars and aeroplanes need petroleum, made from crude oil, to fuel them. Suddenly the rush to find oil was on. By 1932, it was certain that Arabia had oil. Bahrain was the first oil producer but it was not long before oil was found in other places, in much larger quantities. In the last ten years of the twentieth century, it was calculated that Arabia had 65 per cent of the world's oil resources.

?

How is oil formed?

Oil is a fossil fuel. All the places where oil is found were once covered by sea. Tiny sea plants and animals that got their energy from the sun's heat and light sank to the seabed when they died and were covered by tiny particles of rock and minerals called sediment. Over millions of years, the layers of mud and sand turned into rock. As the animals decayed, heat and pressure on them produced oil.

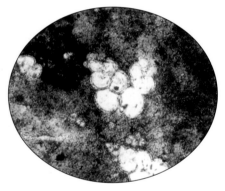

Fossilised plankton

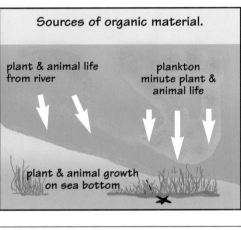

Sources of organic material.

plant & animal life from river

plankton minute plant & animal life

plant & animal growth on sea bottom

?

What are hydrocarbons?

The bodies of plants and animals contain oxygen, hydrogen and carbon. When plankton dies oxygen leaves their bodies and the remaining carbon and hydrogen turns into hydrocarbons. Oil and the natural gas that is often found in pockets above the oil are formed from hydrocarbon remains. Droplets of oil seeped into layered, porous rocks and were held there as a sponge holds drops of water. They were trapped between layers of harder rocks.

The largest reserves are in the Middle East.

Petroleum is found in many parts of the world, but some countries have much larger oil reserves than others. This chart shows proven oil reserves throughout the world. The numbers represent billions of barrels per region.

Middle East
733.9

Oil is measured in barrels.

one barrel contains 159 litres

Asia Pacific
41.1

North America
61.0

S.& Central America
101.2

Africa
112.2

Europe & Eurasia
139.2

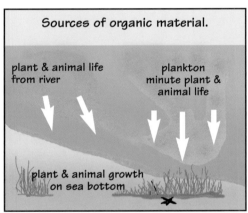

Below, an oilfield in the Oman desert.

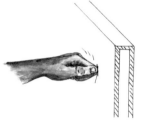

How do geologists know where oil is likely to be found?

Oil companies find and extract crude oil and gas. Today they make use of the full range of modern technology in their search for oil. Satellite maps showing rock types and formations are studied, as well as magnetic surveys from the air. Computers turn this information into pictures of rock structures hundreds, or even thousands, of metres below the surface. Highly skilled geologists study rock formations in the desert or sea, and consult the computer data to decide whether oil or gas are likely to lie beneath the surface. If an area looks promising, a seismic survey is carried out. A series of small explosions are set off beneath the ground and shock waves bouncing off the rocks below are measured.

Geologists interpreting a seismic cross-section.

Listening to the difference between hollow and solid.

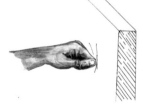

Bang on a hollow wall.

The different echoes that you hear are the same as a those a geologist is listening for when he conducts a seismic survey.

Bang on a solid wall.

If the echoes are very slow coming back, the rock is porous and oil may be present. If the echoes come back very fast, there is no hope of oil being there because the rocks are solid. Measurements identify if the area has porous rocks which can contain fluids. The fluids may be oil, gas or water.

Pore Space

A diagram of porous rocks showing the reservoirs between them.

When was oil first discovered in Arabia?

Pioneer oil explorers relied on guesswork more than on science to find rocks that were likely to contain oil.

One early pioneer was a New Zealander named Frank Holmes, who was working in Bahrain searching for fresh water. He became convinced that oil was present there. He believed also that an immense oilfield ran from Kuwait down the mainland coast of the Arabian Gulf. In reward for his success in finding water, he was given a concession to look for oil in Bahrain. Later he was also awarded concessions to search in eastern Saudi Arabia and Kuwait. But Frank Holmes was not able to take advantage of his concessions as large amounts of money had to be invested in early exploration. It was difficult to find companies prepared to risk this investment. Eventually the concessions were awarded to other companies. On June 1st, 1932 the first oil well began to flow in Bahrain. A new chapter in the history of Arabia began.

Right, one of the first oil wells to be dug, in the Eastern Province of Saudi Arabia.

DISCOVERY OF OIL – DRILLING THE WELLS

The early years spent drilling for oil in the countries of the Arabian peninsula were not easy. The first wells drilled did not produce encouraging results. A great deal of time and money had to be invested in the search for where it lay. However, every country eventually located oil reserves and by 1965 Arabia had replaced the United States of America as the world's largest producer of petroleum. Saudi Arabia's oil company, Aramco, is now the biggest oil producer in the world. Drilling a new well is an expensive and dangerous business but is the only way to confirm whether oil and/or gas are present. All the latest technology is used to extract the maximum amount of oil from each well.

A drilling rig (right) is putting in a well to get oil and gas out of the ground.

Wells no longer go straight into the ground. Once the main shaft of the well is drilled down to the oil, it then branches off in several different directions horizontally. This makes sure that as much of the oil is extracted as possible.

Oil usually flows by itself because it is under pressure and has gas, like a fizzy drink.

When the pressure is low or there is no gas present, oil has to be helped to the surface. A pump can be fitted into the bottom of the well, or gas can be injected into the well to artificially force the oil up. Heavy oil is pumped by a 'nodding donkey'. Sometimes the pump head is made into an amusing character, like this hoopoe bird.

When was oil discovered?

This diagram shows the year that oil was first discovered in each country

1932
BAHRAIN

1938
SAUDI ARABIA
KUWAIT

1940
QATAR

1958
UAE

1964
OMAN

1987
YEMEN

!

FACTOID

A collection of steel valves that controls the flow of oil is called a 'Christmas tree'.

They are put in place once the drilling of the well is complete. The 'Christmas tree' in the picture below is on the site of Bahrain's first oil well.

Many oil wells in Arabia are drilled into the seabed. Offshore production platforms (*above*) often install pipe-lines to the land, where the oil is processed and stored before being piped to tankers.

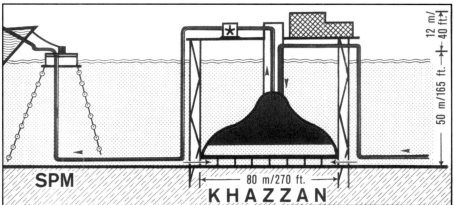

In the waters off Dubai, a unique system was developed so the whole operation could take place offshore. Huge storage vessels were made called *khazzans*, which is the Arabic word for storage. They are shaped like wide-necked glasses, with no bottom and are attached to the seabed with steel piping. They work on the principle that oil and water do not mix. As oil flows into the *khazzan* from the top, water is forced out of the bottom. When oil is withdrawn from the top of the *khazzan* to be pumped aboard tankers, water rises to take its place. Each *khazzan* is taller than a 15-storey building and holds nearly half a million barrels of crude oil.

Thousands of kilometres of pipeline carry the crude oil and gas from onshore wellheads to processing plants. Some is used locally and the rest is stored in tanker terminals on the coast. It is exported to many customers in different parts of the world.

One huge pipeline, called the East-West Crude Oil Pipeline, runs 1,200 kilometres across the width of Saudi Arabia. This one pipeline has the capacity to carry 5 million barrels a day, or roughly twice the amount of crude oil used each day in France.

The oil is pushed through the line by two 'super pumps' at each of the eleven pumping stations along the pipeline. A turbine as powerful as that on a Boeing 747 aircraft drives each pump.

USING THE OIL

Crude oil is a very valuable resource but it must be treated in a refinery before it can be used. It can be refined to make high-energy fuels such as petroleum and diesel oil for use in cars, buses and lorries. Aviation fuel is used in aeroplanes. Machines need oil, called lubricants, to make the parts move smoothly. It is also the raw material of the plastics industry. In the past, most of the objects used in everyday life were made from natural materials found locally. Today these have been largely replaced by objects manufactured from oil.

The letters OPEC stand for Organisation of Petroleum Exporting Countries. Saudi Arabia, Kuwait, Qatar and the United Arab Emirates are members. OPEC set 'quotas' that control how much oil can be produced. This is to make sure that there is a steady flow of oil onto the world markets, neither too little nor too much and a fair price can be obtained for the oil.

How is the crude oil from the ground made suitable for use?

At a refinery, the oil is heated in a furnace to 350°C until it boils and gives off vapour. The vapour is fed to a tall tower where it cools as it rises up the tower. The hydrocarbons in the vapour turn to liquids at different temperatures.

Below, a diagram showing how crude oil is split into gases and oils at different temperatures in the refining tower. Right, a refinery in Qatar.

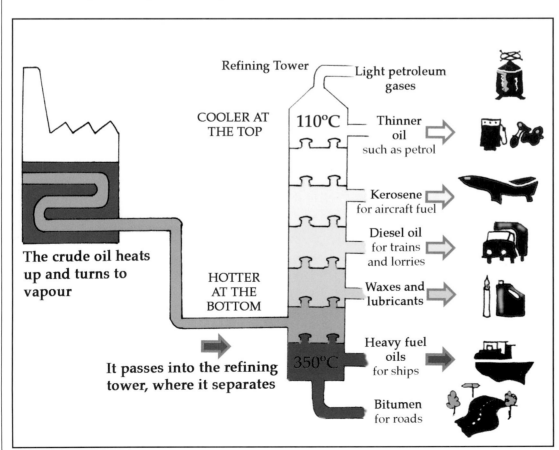

Refining Tower

Light petroleum gases

COOLER AT THE TOP

110°C

Thinner oil such as petrol

Kerosene for aircraft fuel

Diesel oil for trains and lorries

Waxes and lubricants

Heavy fuel oils for ships

Bitumen for roads

The crude oil heats up and turns to vapour

HOTTER AT THE BOTTOM

350°C

It passes into the refining tower, where it separates

Why is natural gas a valuable source of energy?

In recent years, natural gas which is not associated with crude oil has been produced. It is a very valuable source of energy which is clean and leaves no dirty residues. Special heavyweight piping, like that below, is necessary to control high pressures found when drilling for natural gas. Like oil, natural gas has to be treated before it can be used.

FACTOID

Fast cars, boats and planes consume vast quantities of fuel.

A fighter plane may burn 10,000 litres of fuel during each hour of flight.

A Class One petrol engine power boat consumes 280 litres an hour during a race.

Why does oil sometimes cause environmental problems?

Governments of the countries of Arabia and the oil companies themselves have introduced measures to protect the environment. Constant practice ensures that, when a real emergency occurs, everyone is ready to deal with it quickly and efficiently. *Below, a team from the Eastern Province of Saudi Arabia tackle an oil spill.*

MODERN BUILDING MATERIALS & CONSTRUCTION METHODS

In a few short years, after the discovery of oil in the middle of the 20th century, the appearance of Arabia was transformed by the wealth and development that oil money brought with it. As well as an influx of people coming to work in the oil industry itself, an infrastructure of roads, airports and shipping terminals was needed to service it. Buildings to house modern health facilities, schools and universities were all given priority by the rulers so that everyone could benefit from oil wealth. Traditional building materials were replaced with concrete and steel which were quick and easy to use in construction work. Cement, a natural substance made from limestone, was mixed with rock and sand to make concrete. It was quarried throughout Arabia and large quantities were also imported. A huge labour force of architects, engineers and construction workers arrived from other parts of the world to help with the development. By the beginning of the 21st century, the architecture of Arabia had become world famous for its advanced modern styles and 'state of the art' construction techniques.

A busy junction in Qatar's capital, Doha.

Cement has to be mixed with small stones and water to make concrete. It is often sold ready mixed, and is transported in large, drum shaped containers. Concrete is poured when it is wet into the moulds that have been made to receive it.

Concrete has to be given extra strength by inserting a steel cage into it. This is called reinforced concrete. Reinforced concrete was invented by a French gardener named Joseph Monier in 1868. A steel cage is made and surrounded with a wooden mould called shuttering. After the wet concrete is poured into the mould, it is allowed to dry. In one day it becomes dry enough for the shuttering to be removed. However, it takes one month before the concretre reaches its maximum strength.

Cement factories, like that on the left, can be seen in operation throughout Arabia, but much of the cement used is imported.

New highways replaced tracks that had been used for centuries linking towns and villages across the Arabian Peninsula. Journeys that had taken days to do in the past were suddenly shortened to a few hours. This road, linking Riyadh and Dhahran in Saudi Arabia, shows how the past way of life was not forgotten by construction engineers.

In August 2001, the dream of Sheikh Mohammad bin Rashid Al Maktoum to increase the length of coastline of the United Arab Emirates by building an island offshore, became a reality. A most remarkable construction project, to create an island in the shape of a palm tree in the sea, started to take shape. It was to be built using only natural materials.

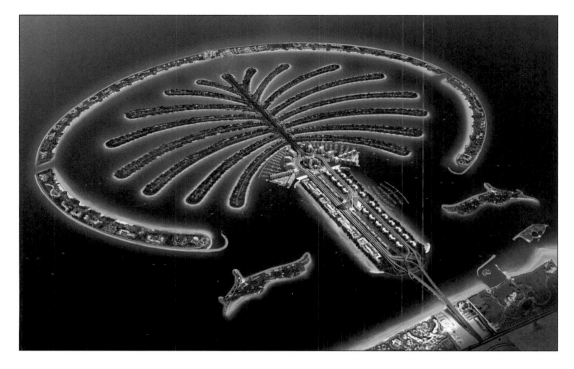

An engineering team, was brought to Dubai from Holland, was chosen because it had experience in reclaiming land from the sea. But at the start of the project no-one knew whether it would be possible to overcome the forces of nature which constantly threatened to destroy the new island.

The massive island was designed to be 5.5 kilometres across. It is visible from space. The first step in the construction process was to construct a breakwater of solid rock, so that the sand from which the island was built would not wash away as soon as it was put in place. The stone wall had to be strong enough to last for centuries.

Palm Island, Dubai

FACTOID

It took 5.5 million cubic metres of rock to build the horse-shoe shaped breakwater, which was needed to protect the island. It stands 3 metres high above the waves, and is 11.5 kilometres long. This amount of rock would be enough to build two Egyptian pyramids. The breakwater was completed in August, 2003.

As the breakwater grew in size, sand foundations for the island were laid below sea-level. 94 million cubic metres of sand were needed, which would be enough sand to cover the whole of Manhattan 1 metre deep.

A method of dredging sand from another part of the sea-bed and bringing it to the place where it is needed is known as 'rainbowing'. Dredgers scooped up sand, and then sprayed it, like the arc of a rainbow, into position. 676 kilometres up in space a satellite called Iconos took pictures of the island as it was being formed to check that the sand was being put in the correct place. In October 2003, Palm Island was ready for the houses, hotels and shopping malls that were to be constructed on it.

Two further Palm Islands have now been constructed, along with The World, which is a complex of 300 small islands which will take the shape of the world. New ways of building and the ability of engineers to conquer the forces of nature have certainly been pushed to new and exciting limits in Arabia.

SUPERSTRUCTURES

As new technology developed, the use of iron and steel opened up the possibilities of constructing large buildings of great height and strength. The challenge of producing grander and more imaginative buildings meant that practical problems using new materials and methods of construction had to be solved. In some buildings the main framework is hidden away by an outer covering of lightweight material. Skyscrapers can even look as though they are made from glass. In others, a white Teflon fabric can imitate the flow of curves so that buildings no longer have hard edges. Some new buildings have such special qualities of beauty or style that they stand out from the others, and become landmarks in their city.

Cleaning tall buildings. Abseilers swing out from dizzying heights, water jets in hand, to clean the sail wall on another unusual building in Dubai, the Creek Golf Club.

Enormous cranes capable of lifting the weight of 40 Range Rovers can be seen working on new buildings.

FACTOID

The **Burj Al Arab,** in Dubai, appears in the Guiness Book of Records in 2001 as the tallest hotel in the world. The Eiffel Tower in Paris and Burj Al Arab are the same height at 321 metres. The sail wall of the Burj Al Arab is made from double-skinned Teflon, coated with glass fibre. The sail symbolises Arabia's connections with the sea.

Two new skyscrapers, under construction in 2006, aim to be even taller than the Burj Al Arab. It is not yet known the full height of Al Burj and Burj Dubai until construction is completed but they will be among the world's tallest buildings.

The Hajj terminal at Jeddah, Saudi Arabia, (above) from where pilgrims can travel on the annual pilgrimage to Makkah, was completed in 1982. Three million pilgrims are expected annually through the terminal, which is so large that it can comfortably hold 80,000 pilgrims. It is 25 per cent larger than the world's largest office building, the Pentagon in Washingtcn DC, USA.

The Faisaliah Tower (left) is owned by the King Faisal Foundation, and was the first skyscraper to be built in Riyadh, Saudi Arabia. It stands 267 metres high and was completed in 2000. A stunning show with fireworks and lasers that lit up the night sky presented the tower to an amazed audience, estimated to be a quarter of a million people.

Traditional low skylines have been replaced by tall majestic buildings in large cities throughout Arabia reflecting the modernity and wealth of the area.

Below, one of the many towering office/residential buildings in Deira, Dubai, with its own helipad.

A combination of traditional and ultra-modern techniques won the Aga Khan Award for Tuwaiq Palace (below) at Riyadh, Saudi Arabia. The award is given for architectural excellence throughout the Muslim world.

The building gives the appearance of a fort surrounded by an encampment of tents. Inside the tents, constructed from Teflon-coated fibreglass cloth, are halls for receptions and sports. The 'fort' is a thick, high wall providing rooms for guests. Tuwaiq Palace cost $31.2 million dollars to build. When the building was awarded its prize, the judges noted how perfectly it blends into the desert landscape.

GLOSSARY

ahlan wa sahlan	welcome
Allah	God
arak rak	Toothbrush plant
areesh	house made from palm fronds
arta	plant with useful properties (e.g. curing hides)
bangari moshook	bracelet with spikes or triangular stones
bakhur	see *dukhan*
barchan	crescent-shaped sand dunes
barjeel	tower for funelling wind through a house
basal	onion
bedouin (bedu)	people of the desert
berberi	pearls
bisht	fine cloak, usually of silk
boom	type of dhow
burqa	face mask
da'an	palm frond panels used to construct walls
dhub	lizard
dukhan	incense cakes, also known as *bakhur*
egmesh	red cloth used to wrap pearls in holiday at end of Ramadan
falaj	chanelled water distribution system
ghaf	evergreen tree found in sandy areas
ghoutra/shemag	white headdress
haban	wild oleaner;goatskin bag
hadrah	type of fish trap
Hajj	pilgrimage to Makkah, one of the Five Pillars of Islam
hijra	the migration of the Prophet Muhammad to Medina in AD 622
hirz	box attached to a necklace
ihram	seamless garment worn by pilgrims on the *Hajj*
'iqal	twisted blackcoil to hold a headdress in place; camel hobble
jambia	curved dagger (Yemen)
jelbut	type of dhow
jerz	small axe from Shihuh
jird	species of gerbil
juss	part of the palm tree
Ka'bah	Islam's most important shrine in Makkah
kanah	Eyelash plant
kandoora	flowing white gown
khanjar	curved dagger (Oman)
khazzan	storage vessel for crude oil and gases
kohl	eyeshadow
Kiswah	embroidered cloth which covers the *Ka'bah*
Koran	see *Qu'ran*
kuma	embroidered cap
lateen	type of sail

majlis	meeting room
manqalah	protective glove worn by a falconer
mashrabiyya	decorative latticework of a traditional wooden window
muezzin	caller of the prayer (from the minaret)
mihrab	prayer niche showing the direction of the Ka'bah
mikhla	hawking bag
minbar	carved staircase, mosque pulpit
mu'allim	teacher
mumtasha	necklace
murtash	trembling
nacre	cells in an oyster's body which make the shell
nahham	musician
nakhuda	master of a ship
oud	stringed instrument
oudh	type of wood used as perfume
qaffal	the journey home
qibla	the Makkah-facing wall of a mosque
Qu'ran (Koran)	holy book of Islam
rahmani	book used for navigation
Ramadan	holy month
reeshah	palm leaves looking like feathers
rheem	sand gazelle
sa'af	house built from the complete palm frond
sabkha	salt flat
saffee	rabbitfish
saluki	hunting dog
sambuk	pearling boat
sarouj	locally made cement
shamal	strong north wind
sharee	local name for an Emperor fish
shashah	boat constructed from palm fronds
sheikh	tribal leader
shemagh	white or checked headdress
shisha	water pipe
shuwa	traditional oven
simr	acacia tree
souq	shop, market
subuq	rope attached to a falcon's ankles
tawwah	pearl merchant
thobe	gown
tilwah	lure for training falcons
umm an nar	Bronze Age culture
wadi	riverbed
wakir	falcon's perch
wasm	brand used on camels
zakat	alms to the poor, one of the Five Pillars of Islam
zoolie	toilet (on board a dhow)

INDEX